Why Reading Literature in School Still Matters:
Imagination, Interpretation, Insight

Why Reading Literature in School Still Matters:
Imagination, Interpretation, Insight

DENNIS J. SUMARA
University of Alberta

LAWRENCE ERLBAUM ASSOCIATES, PUBLISHERS
Mahwah, New Jersey   London

2002

Lawrence Erlbaum Associates, Inc., Publishers
10 Industrial Avenue
Mahwah, NJ 07430

Cover design by Kathryn Houghtaling Lacey
Cover photo from the author's personal collection.

Library of Congress Cataloging-in-Publication Data

Sumara, Dennis J., 1958–
Why reading literature in school still matters : imagination,
    interpretation, insight / Dennis J. Sumara.
    p. cm.
    Includes bibliographical references and index.
    ISBN 0-8058-4228-4 (cloth : alk. paper) — ISBN 0-8058-4229-2
    (paper : alk. paper)
    1. Reading. 2. Literature—Study and teaching. 3. Reader-response
    criticism. I. Title.
LB1050.2 .S86 2002
807´.1–dc21   2002019866

Books published by Lawrence Erlbaum Associates are printed on acid-
free paper, and their bindings are chosen for strength and durability.

Printed in the United States of America
10 9 8 7 6 5 4 3 2

for my teachers

Contents

The memories we elude catch up to us, overtake us like a shadow. A truth appears suddenly in the middle of a thought, a hair on a lens.

Anne Michaels, *Fugitive Pieces*

Preface

In this book, I argue that reading literature can be a focal practice that creates the possibility for deep insight. Like the gardener who cares about her garden, the reader who is interested in creating insight must develop a dedicated attention to the work at hand, understanding that the immediate products are not necessarily the most important ones. Acts of reading deeply, like the acts of cultivating, nurturing, and tending that are part of gardening, generate knowledge that transcends the acts themselves.

The title for this book, *Why Reading Literature in School Still Matters: Imagination, Interpretation, Insight,* represents two important ideas. First, it points to the ways literary engagements can facilitate the creation of interesting sites for thinking. Second, it suggests that the enterprise of public schooling is still an important social project. Because schools support intergenerational relationships developed explicitly around representing, imagining, and interpreting knowledge, they continue to function as important sites for creating insights into human experience. By creating pedagogical structures that include shared interpretations of literary engagements, I believe schools can continue to push the boundaries of what is considered true about the world.

The thesis of this book is both profoundly simple and exceedingly complex. I argue that literary engagements, and the practices of interpretation that are conditioned by those engagements, can become useful ways for people not only to maintain a sense of personal coherence but, as well, to expand their imagined world of possibilities. Although this book presents a theoretical argument about the value of literary engagement, it is also a book that is meant to provide practical advice for teachers who want to reconceptualize their use of literary texts in school contexts.

I have been thinking about the ideas presented in this book for many years. As I read the final draft of this manuscript, I wondered why I continue to feel compelled to promote practices of close reading and deep interpretation in a world that offers many of its citizens access to unbelievable amounts of information. By typing a few "keywords" into an Internet search engine, I can access information on almost any topic. However, as I argue throughout this book, access to information does not guarantee understanding, nor does it necessarily create the conditions for deep insight. Understanding requires interpretation, and interpretation depends on learned practices. Reading literature in school still matters because it creates opportunities for such practices to be learned. This does not mean that all students who engage in these literary interpretive practices will continue to do so throughout their lives. However, it does mean—at the very least—that they will have learned one structure that assists in the development of deep insight into their own experiences, and the ways these continue to be influenced by history and by present context. As Anne Michaels (1996) suggests in her novel *Fugitive Pieces*, learning how to develop insight is important:

> If you know one landscape well, you will look at all other landscapes differently. And if you learn to love one place, sometimes you can also learn to love another. (p. 82)

In this book, I argue that literary experience is a place. By learning to attend to its details, readers can improve the quality of their lived experiences.

Because I hope the reader will consider this book a "commonplace" for interpretation, I have left large margins and plenty of white spaces for "notes." I hope the reader will be willing to engage with ideas presented in this book by scribbling notes in the margins. As with any collection of personal memorabilia, the traces of responses found in a book can generate an interesting commonplace for interpretation. These traces become even more interesting if more than one reader creates them. Therefore, I hope that readers of this book might be willing to pass their annotated copies of the book to other readers. In so doing, the texts will more explicitly begin to function as historical documents that bear not only a trace of the author's thinking, but a record of different readers' engagements with it.

In order to represent some of the complexity of literary engagements, I have written this book using two styles of writing. Five of the chapters are developed using familiar expository prose (Chapters 1, 2, 4, 6, and 8). The others are more explicitly performative (Chapters 3, 5, and 7). The performative chapters are intended to foreground how language and written representations of language create organizing structures for imagining, creating, and interpreting human identities. As the reader identifies with aspects of the text, and develops a relationship between these identifications and the context of reading, a complex web of associations emerges. The performative chapters aim to represent aspects of this associational complexity. At the same time, they also aim to advance the argument presented throughout the book. Although I do not claim that these performative pieces are forms of literary fiction, I have created them so that they might remind readers of what it is like to be involved with literary fiction.

In Chapter One, I provide a brief biography of experiences that led to the development of ideas presented in the chapters that follow. I use the phrase "the gradual instant" to represent how insight emerging from literary engagement resembles geographical transformation. Although it is not always apparent, large shifts in thinking, like large changes in the natural world, are always preceded by a complex choreography of small changes. This helps us to understand why it is sometimes necessary to develop sustained and close relationships with literary texts, over time, if deep insight is to be generated.

In Chapter Two, I introduce the use of the "Commonplace Book" as a strategy for developing deep insight with literary texts by referring to research I conducted with teachers who read Michael Ondaatje's (1992) novel *The English Patient*, and with grade five and six children who read Lois Lowry's (1993) novel *The Giver*. In addition to reviewing literatures that provide a new vocabulary for thinking about literary engagements, the chapter offers a beginning framework for understanding literary relations as important sites for human learning.

In Chapter Three, I present the first performative chapter. In this chapter I aim to represent the complexity of the reader's interpretive relations with literary texts and with contexts of reading. Specifically, I try to show how literary engagements can provide necessary interruptions to cultural commonsense and to daily routines. I call this writing "troubling bodies" since it shows how biological bodies, literary and theoretical bodies of knowledge, and cultural collective bodies continually intersect with one another. Although I suggest that these bodies can be troubling, I also hint at the importance of making trouble. As I will elaborate in the next chapter, human perception needs to be interrupted in order for it to become better able to attend to the often-unnoticed details of daily life.

Calling into question commonsense views of identity creation, which conceive of the subject as predestined or socially constructed, Chapter Four offers a complex view of identity that is supported by research in evolutionary biology, neuroscience, and ecology. Using examples from my engagements with Mem Fox's (1984) children's picture book, *Wilfrid Gordon McDonald Partridge*, this chapter interprets the complex relations of memory, cultural objects and narrative practices, including practices of reading and interpretation.

Chapter Five attempts to show how literary engagement can be conceptualized as a form of human science research. In this writing I demonstrate how I applied literary anthropological research methods to my readings of Anne Michael's (1996) novel *Fugitive Pieces* in order to interpret a historical relationship to my ancestors, focusing on my parents' emergence from events of World War II. These literary engagements are interpreted using historical, philosophical, and theoretical literatures concerned with analyzing relationships among history, memory, culture, geography, language, and identity. In addition to these textual artifacts, I examined personal objects to show how human identity is organized by cultural artifacts and, as well, how these develop new significance when understood in relation to emergent cultural knowledge.

In Chapter Six I use insights from my reading of Martha Brook's (1997) young adult novel *Bone Dance* to argue that human emotion and attachment are learning experiences. By suggesting that experiences of love are made, not found, I highlight the complex ways discursive practices create identities and identifications. From this perspective, loving attachments are conceptualized as developing through processes of attention and discernment. I suggest that practices of mindfulness, such as the close reading of a literary text, can assist human subjects to learn how to create loving attachments to ideas, to landscapes, to practices, and to people.

Chapter Seven develops an elaborated understanding of embodied reading. Linked to recent research studies from evolutionary biology and neuroscience, insights from my engagement with Mark Salzman's (2000) novel *Lying Awake* demonstrate how human subjects require focused practices in mindfulness in order to develop perceptive and interpretive abilities. When linked to my memories of attending a Catholic retreat as a high school student, and descriptions of interpretation practices I use with my undergraduate students in teacher education, these theoretical insights support the development of ritualized imagination and interpretation practices within school contexts.

Chapter Eight suggests that practices of attentive reading and writing create important conditions for the development of personal and cultural insight. I argue that in order for literature to matter in school, theories of learning that insist on excavating "truth" or representing commonsense must be abandoned. I do not argue that literature study must become primary in school settings. Instead, I suggest that practices of literary engagement and interpretation can offer insight into ways in which human societies and cultures might interrupt the familiarity of commonsense and, at the same time, create conditions for other creative and imaginative practices.

The Gradual Instant

1

CHAPTER ONE

Earlier this year I re-read Margaret Laurence's (1964) novel *The Stone Angel*. Presented as the autobiography of elderly Hagar Shipley, this story shows how life evolves as a surprise, not a plan. Most striking in this novel is the way Laurence is able to reveal the complex topography that conditions profound insight. For 90-year-old Hagar, such insight emerges from what Anne Michaels (1996), in her novel *Fugitive Pieces*, describes as "the gradual instant":

> Nothing is sudden. Not an explosion—planned, timed, wired carefully—not the burst door. Just as the earth invisibly prepares its cataclysms, so history is the gradual instant. (p. 77)

Near the end of her life, when Hagar realizes Marvin has been the best son, not John, it is an epiphany that has been years in the making. As with all unexpected revelations, there is no immediate accounting for this understanding. For Hagar, insight does not spring directly from a particular episode in her life, but emerges ambiguously from the strange crevices that collect memory, current perception, and fantasy. That she now is able to express her affection for Marvin is significant not because it is a more truthful account of her feelings, but because it helps her to improve the quality of her life.

Hagar's experience is not unique. It is only in retrospect that we are able to interpret our lives and imbue them with meaning. *memor* Making explicit these interpretations is the primary work of memoirs, ethnographies, and autobiographies. That is why I read them. I do not read them for pleasure, although I do experience pleasure. I do not read them to learn moral lessons, although I do learn moral lessons. I do not read them to expand my repertoire of cultural and historical knowledge, although this does happen. I read them because I find I must continually create new sites to interpret my lived situation. I read them because I have learned that what is considered true about myself and my contexts is not easily accessed or represented. Truth does not exist in platitudes and clichés or moral imperatives. Truth cannot be found, directly, by asking others for advice, or from reading pop-psychology books that give directions for improved living conditions. What is experienced as truthful emerges from the complex relations of history, memory, language, and geography.

Like other educators who are interested in understanding the relationship between questions of knowledge and identity (e.g., Ellsworth, 1997; Greene, 1995; Miller, 1990; Willinksy, 1998), I have abandoned the idea that universal truths exist. What is considered true about experience is not foundational to experience, nor does it exist outside experience. There are no grand narratives that can adequately represent the complexity of human perception and understanding. Even so, human beings are compelled to try to interpret experience. Following arguments made by Rorty (1989, 1999), I have come to believe that the quest for essences and foundations must cease. Instead, I have become committed to emphasizing the importance of insight. And, like others who are interested in writing about insight (e.g., Grumet, 1988; DeSalvo, 1996) I have learned that it cannot be discovered. Instead, insight is fashioned from what François Lyotard (1984) has called "les petits récits"—the "small stories."

What I am describing is not an original idea. As ethnographers and novelists know, what is interesting to people are not the big ideas that are believed to organize human experience. More interesting are the tiny plots and descriptions that circumscribe past, present and projected worlds of experience. Created from these small stories, sometimes, is what we humans recognize as insight, as revelation, as something that prompts us to remark: "Yes! That's so true! I love you. I hate you. I'm sorry."

Although small insights occur daily ("If I use the right lane,

I will move through this traffic more quickly."), deep insight is not so easily gained. Deep insight emerges from the hard work of interpreting one's relations with people, to objects people have made (including narratives that describe and explain experience), and to the more-than-human world. Although conditions for the production of insight can be created, deep insight is usually surprising, occurring unexpectedly, emerging from curious places.

One of these curious places is what we have come to call "imagination." As Jerome Bruner (1986) has suggested, imaginative thought is supported by the use of subjunctive forms of language. In the English language, words like "might," "could," "would," "should," are used to convey a sense of future possibility or obligation. To imagine, then, is to create interpreted bridges between what is held in memory, what currently exists, and what is predicted about the future. From this perspective, imagining is not a special act limited to certain persons or certain situations. Rather, imagining is central to human cognition (Egan, 1997). As I argue throughout this book, it is possible to create conditions for the expansion of imaginative thought. In the chapters that follow, I aim to show how literary interpretation practices can transform imaginative occasions into productive insights.

My personal reading experiences have been influential in helping me develop some of the theories and practices presented in this book. For example, over the past 25 years I have read *The Stone Angel* three times. Each reading experience has been differently situated, conducted for different purposes, and has yielded different interpretations and effects. When I read it in 1976, I was an undergraduate student of Canadian literature. I recall little of that reading, other than my attraction to Hagar's strong personality and my interest in the world of the elderly—which, at that point in my life, seemed exotic, not pending. When I re-read it in 1999, I did so in response to my reading of James King's (1997) biography of Margaret Laurence and a desire to remember and interpret my young adulthood. As I became reacquainted with Hagar Shipley, a generous interpretive site was created, one that connected my recent interpretations of Margaret Laurence via King's autobiography with my current situation as an academic researching literary engagement.

My third reading of *The Stone Angel* was prompted by an unexpected tourist opportunity. During a recent cross-Canada trek from Toronto to Edmonton to take new positions at the University of Alberta, my partner and I happened to pass through Neepawa, Manitoba, which, as the sign at the entrance to the town reminded us, was the long-time home of Margaret Laurence. Although we forgot to travel to the cemetery to look for the "stone angel," we did locate her former house. Viewing it from the idling van was reassuring to me: the house is substantial, two storied, and verandahed—a place with plenty of space for thinking.

As we drove through this small town in the middle of the Canadian prairies, I was reminded of how extraordinary products can emerge from seemingly ordinary places. How could Margaret Laurence have written such brilliant prose in this place? But then I remembered that she spent years in Africa and England. If a sense of "place" includes memory, then for Laurence the town of Neepawa was a much more textured and interesting context for writing than could ever be noticed by a passing stranger like myself.

During that first week in Edmonton my energies were consumed with the intense labor associated with redistributing life into a different context. When I finally located the copy of *The Stone Angel* I had purchased in 1999 (unfortunately, my first copy seems to have vanished), I noticed that included at the back of the novel is an "afterword" written in 1988 by Laurence's friend and colleague, Adele Wiseman. I had not noticed this in my previous reading. This time I read it first. Woven throughout this text are excerpts from letters Laurence wrote to Wiseman during her work on *The Stone Angel*. Here is my favorite passage:

> This book (?) of mine, you see, has been written almost entirely without conscious thought, & although the conscious thought will enter into the re-writing, on the first time through I simply put down the story as the old lady told it to me (so to speak) & let it go where it wanted, & only when I was halfway through did I realize how it all tied together & what the theme was. I didn't know it had a theme before, nor did I know the purpose or meaning of some of the events & objects in the story, until gradually it became clear. (p. 314)

The gradual instant. Over time, with persistence and the use of interpretive strategies and writing techniques, the pattern becomes evident, the theme emerges, and what is identified as meaning is presented. This is what happens when one becomes involved in what I call, following the work of Albert Borgmann (1992), "focal practices." The practice of gardening, the writing of poetry or novel or memoir, the writing and singing of songs, the inventing of new forms of mathematics—all these can function as sites within which personal and cultural interpretive work can be accomplished. That Laurence should not know precisely what her novel is about until quite late in the process represents the way in which one cannot understand the particularity of one's lived experiences easily or immediately. It seems that there is no direct correspondence, through language, between experience and interpretations of experience. One cannot say simply, fully or unambiguously what one's life is or what one means.

This does not suggest, however, that humans should not attempt to interpret their experiences or to make those interpretations available to others. As I try to show in the chapters that follow, interpretation practices function to create experiences of self-identity. As a species that has learned to use language and its many forms as tools to connect ourselves to the human, human made, and more-than-human world, we must continue to create interesting interpretive sites that both clarify and complicate what we believe to be true.

Of course, what I am describing is not unknown. Margaret Laurence developed her abilities as a writer of prose fiction in order to create such interpretive spaces. Although I do not believe she is writing about herself when she presents the narrative of Hagar Shipley, there is no doubt, from what she says about her experience of writing (see King, 1999), that she is developing personal insight through writing novels. In writing about another character with whom she becomes relationally involved, the writer is altered. As Margaret invents Hagar, Hagar also participates in the continued invention of Margaret.

These experiences are not confined to those who craft literary fiction. Other literary workers, such as critics and biographers, have presented similar insights about their experiences. In her memoir *Vertigo*, Louise DeSalvo (1996) writes about her years of researching the life of Virginia Woolf:

> She has been very good to me, this woman. And, in time, it is through her life that I begin to understand the lives of the women in my family—my mother's, my sister's. And finally, mine. (p. 241)

Insight also emerges from involvement in other aesthetic practices. In Jane Urquhart's (2001) historical novel *The Stone Carver*, the main character, Walter Allward, a master stone carver commissioned to create a monument to the soldiers who died at Vimy Ridge, describes his experience working on this project:

I have been eating and sleeping stone for so long it has become an obsession with me. And, incidentally, a nightmare. (p. 270)

Here, Allward shows how involvement in any creative art form becomes an organizing structure for one's sense of self-identity. Importantly, while these aesthetic involvements can become personally rewarding, they can also become terribly difficult. Because the making of art requires more than simple representation but also, as Gadamer (1990) has suggested, a re-presenting, the work of the artist is to continually find ways to interrupt familiar perceptions and interpretations. This, in itself, can become troubling, since interrupting familiarity in a particular aspect of one's experience is influential to all other aspects.

Challenging familiar perceptions is difficult. As Madeleine Grumet (1991a) explains, "The problem with everyday life is that it is always the ground, rarely the figure" (p. 75). Artful living requires that elements of unnoticed life be re-surfaced, re-examined, and re-presented. This is not only work for people who make art objects. It is work for anyone who is interested in continuing to develop deep insight into human experiences.

The discussions of literary engagement presented in this book are developed around a theory of learning that conceptualizes human identity as co-evolving with the production of knowledge. Identity is not some essential quality of the individual human subject. Identity emerges from relationships, including relationships people have with books and other communicative technologies based on language.

Through the invention of languages that can be reproduced and represented in many ways, human beings have learned to create personal and cultural identities that are more complex than those of other species. Literacy practices have become tools to make associations and to preserve personal and cultural memories. The development of computer-assisted electronic communication has expanded these possibilities, offering human beings many more opportunities for identification with others and their ideas than at any other time in history.

Opportunities for identifications, however, do not guarantee that meaningful relationships to people or to their ideas will occur. As I write this, I am reminded of the difficulty a friend of mine has experienced using the Internet to develop a primary relationship. Although she has participated in many contacts and exchanges, possibilities for other-than-electronic relations seem to dissolve once photos are exchanged, or telephone conversations are initiated, or face-to-face meetings are arranged.

While it seems that relational identifications can be maintained through electronically mediated literacy practices, they cannot always continue when the boundaries of these interactions are transgressed. This, in itself, is not problematic if the interlocutors are content to develop a relationship that exists in language, mediated through literacy practices of reading and writing. Similar to how Louise DeSalvo's ongoing relationship with Virginia Woolf continues to be supported through reading and writing interpretation practices, my friend's Internet relations can be maintained when these are contained within the organizing structures of that genre of interaction. The difficulty, it seems, is that while they mimic the experiential structures of literary engagement, on-line relations hold the promise for other kinds of intimacy, including physical contact, while literary engagements do not. The literary relationship remains as imagination and fantasy, and can become incorporated into the reader's daily life without the usual commitments or obligations required by many other types of relationships.

It is not only electronically mediated social relations that become difficult when the boundaries of their initial organizational structures are transgressed by face-to-face encounters. Readers' relations with characters and with other people often undergo tension when the initial organizing conditions and structures are changed. Such has been my experience, for example, with authors of books I have read. Because I like to re-read favorite books, I sometimes develop strong identifications with whom Eco (1994) calls the "model author"—the persona the reader invents to represent the flesh and blood author. With books I come to love, these model authors attain mythical status, becoming fantastical, larger than life.

In the past, I have made an effort to meet and become acquainted with the flesh and blood person who has written these books I love. Most of the time, this creates an interpretive problem since, of course, the persona I meet is not the persona I have come to know through identifications with her or his text. The experience is usually disappointing, since I am confronted with evidence that there is often little or no relationship between what one writes and how this is communicated to readers, and how people present themselves, in person, to others. This is why I now resist trying to meet the authors I read, preferring, in most instances, to live within the interpretive structures conditioned by my identifications with what they have written.

In my previous book *Private Readings in Public: Schooling the Literary Imagination* (1996) I outlined a theory of reading that described how engagements with literary fiction participate in the reader's complex ecology of human/human, human/text, human/context relations. Although I supported and developed Rosenblatt's (1978) and Iser's (1978) analyses of the relational experiences of reader/text involvement, I elaborated these by attending to literatures emerging from science and ecology, which interpret relationships between human thinking and biological and ecological systems. Supporting this theoretical framework were a number of analyses of readers' experiences with literary fictions, drawn primarily from work I had done with English teachers and secondary school students. I attempted to show the complex and nuanced ways relations with literary characters, plots, and settings function to create interpretive opportunities for readers.

In this book, I elaborate my earlier theoretical discussions by showing how literary engagements contribute significantly to the ongoing invention of the reading subject. I choose the term "reading subject" to signify that acts of literary engagement create opportunities for both the continued invention of the reader and the ongoing production of knowledge that occurs during acts of reading and interpretation. Drawing from research I have conducted over the past decade with different groups of adult, young adult, and child readers, as well as personal memories of teaching and reading experiences, I attempt to show how literary engagement can become an important site for the ongoing interpretation of the personal, the communal, and the cultural.

Although I emphasize engagements with literary fiction, I acknowledge that these are not the only forms of imaginative encounters that have the potential to produce insight. One interesting example, which resembles the experience of literary engagement, was the overwhelming public response to the sudden death of Diana, Princess of Wales. As I watched the incredible outpouring of grief, and listened to testimonials by persons from all around the world, it became clear to me that many people had developed strong relational identifications with someone they had never met. Their relationship to Diana was wholly developed through the countless media representations of her. This does not mean, however, that the grief people experienced was not real. It does show, however, that what counts as an identity and identification depends more upon narrative structures than physical contact.

The experience of loss is common with readers of literary texts. The research in reader response is replete with examples of how readers mourn the loss of relational identification with characters when their reading of a novel is complete (e.g., Appleyard, 1990; Nell, 1988; Sumara, 1996). As I discuss in greater detail later, because identity emerges from our relations with others, when a relationship ends (whether in divorce, death, or other sudden partings) individuals experience a profound and lingering grief. The grieving, it is important to realize, is not only for what can be identified as the other person, but, as well, for the complex ways in which the relationship with that person has contributed to the development of the identities of the other individuals involved. When my relationship with someone ends, I do not only experience a loss for that person, I experience a loss of personal identity. In order to regain some sense of personal coherence, interpretation practices need to be employed. In the case of Diana's sudden death, the weeklong processes and rituals of public grieving, culminating in the ritual of burial, facilitated the creation of a context for this interpretive work. With literary identifications, practices of re-reading can alleviate experiences of loss, as can opportunities for explicit interpretation of the literary relationship and its possible effects.

Although I sometimes use the word "coherence" to describe a sense of self, I do not mean to suggest that human identities are clearly bounded, predetermined, or fixed. Following post-structural theories of language that emphasize the complex ways humans continually stitch together relationships between language and experience, I understand that human identities are continually in the process of becoming and are never "finished." Even after the death of the biological body, narratives representing the deceased continue to evolve. When I suggest that an identity is coherent, I am arguing that it has a sufficiently identifiable form that can be interpreted. As these practices of identification and interpretation occur, the shape and form of the identity in question continues to evolve and adapt itself to a new interpretive context.

It is important for me to mention that while this book concerns itself with the experience of literary engagement, it is not a book of literary criticism. Furthermore, although I use theoretical tools used by cultural anthropologists, philosophers, ecologists, and cognitive scientists, I am not doing anthropology or philosophy or ecology or cognitive science. Instead, I position myself as someone who works within the field of curriculum studies, with a specific interest in the experience of reading literature in school settings.

As my colleagues and I have discussed elsewhere (Davis, Sumara, & Luce-Kapler, 2000), what distinguishes curriculum studies from other disciplines is its explicit interest in analyzing the relationships among language, culture, learning, and teaching. Implicit in announcing myself as interested in the study of curriculum is my personal history of involvement with persons and ideas in this area and, as well, my commitment to using a wide variety of tools to help me better understand what it means to learn and teach. Although I am interested in this question generally (that is, How do humans learn?) I am also interested in it specifically (What does it mean for students and teachers to read literary texts together?). My involvement in curriculum studies has been strongly influenced by my involvement in the field of "reader-response," a discipline historically linked to the larger fields of literary criticism and reading theory. While the former primarily emerges from university Departments of English, and the latter primarily from Psychology and Education, the field of reader response, historically, has been structured by an interdisciplinary approach to the study of literary engagement (Beach, 1993).

My inquiries into experiences of literary engagement, while depending to a large extent on theoretical tools from other disciplines, must be considered a study of human learning. I situate myself with those theorists who would align themselves with Rorty's (1989) definition of the anti-essentialist. Like Rorty, I do not believe that knowledge can exist in any sort of non-mediated way. For humans, the primary form of mediation is language use. And for most world citizens, language use has become strongly influenced and shaped by various literacy practices.

I develop my arguments about the value of literary engagement through a series of chapters that describe and interpret the lived experiences of these engagements. Each chapter attempts to demonstrate how particular insights can be produced through interpreted literary encounters. Emerging from research-based and other writing I have done over the past decade, I develop my analyses by trying to describe qualities and situations that seem to have interested humans across eras, cultures, languages, social classes, races and genders for centuries. How does one create an identity that is interesting to one's self and to others? What does it mean to know one's family and cultural history? What is the process and meaning of grieving for loved ones? What conditions create meaningful and creative work? What does it mean to learn to fall in love? What does it mean to live within categories of race, class, gender, sexuality and ethnicity?

I invite the reader of this book to participate with me in the exploration of some of the questions announced in this book. I admit that some of the writing—particularly the "performative chapters"—is challenging. Links between ideas are subtle rather than obvious. The reviewers of an earlier draft of this book were concerned that I was demanding too much of the reader, that perhaps I ought to be clearer and more explicit in my final interpretations. In the end, I have decided to be faithful to my subject and allow these indeterminacies to continue. However, I have been deliberately explicit about some issues. Because I hope to create a new understanding of why literature still matters, I understand that I must follow Rorty's (1999) suggestion:

> One way to change instinctive emotional reactions is to provide new language that will facilitate new reactions. By 'new language' I mean not just new words but also creative misuses of language—familiar words used in ways that initially sound crazy. (p. 204)

Although I understand that some of what I am arguing seems a bit crazy, I hope that these ideas might help illuminate why reading literature still matters, especially in school settings. Like Rorty, I believe that theoretical work ought to facilitate a continued hopefulness for human beings and the societies they form and the institutions they create. Because I continue to be hopeful about the possibilities for public schooling, and because I feel strongly about how literary engagements can condition the production of important insights, I believe that reading literature in schools still matters.

CHAPTER TWO

A few years ago I learned that what I had been doing for most of my life could become an interesting form of research. As part of a larger project with high school English teachers, I organized a group that read and discussed Michael Ondaatje's (1992) novel *The English Patient*. While involved in this literary experience, the teachers and I noticed two things—one obvious, the other less so: reading a common literary text can create opportunities to interpret personal and collective experience, and re-reading that text can generate surprising and purposeful insights.

This latter point is also demonstrated through the novel itself, in the English Patient's practice of carrying with him, through all his travels, a frequently read copy of Herodotus's *The Histories*. Although this book is formally known as an account of the war between the Greeks and the Persians in the 4th Century B.C.E., for the English Patient it becomes what he calls a "Commonplace Book" that assists him with ongoing personal reflection. Over a period of thirty years he has added notes, drawn maps of his travels, described love interests, asked questions, and inserted tokens and mementos into his copy of *The Histories*, making it a text different from any other copy that exists.

Informed by insights emerging from our reading of *The English Patient*, our group decided that rather than immediately moving on to the next novel on our list, we would re-read it. We also decided that we would try to create our own Commonplace Books from our copies of *The English Patient* by continuing to inscribe our responses into our texts. As our second reading progressed we found that re-reading and annotating *The English Patient* created a generous space for interpretation. Most interesting were the ways in which our annotations rendered materially present for us the evolutions in our perceptions, and the way these contributed to interpretations of our remembered experiences. By elaborating our relationship to this literary work through re-reading practices, and by trying to symbolize this relationship in writing and in discussions with other readers, we generated an interesting "commonplace" for interpretation.

Two years later I initiated a research project with Dolores van der Wey and her Grade 5/6 class that utilized some of the practices learned from my inquiry with the high school English teachers and my work with *The English Patient*. Using Lois Lowry's (1993) novel *The Giver* as a common class text, we developed a six-week novel study that was structured by Commonplace Book principles and practices.

The Giver depicts a futuristic society where historical and cultural memory is concealed from all but one citizen—the Receiver of Memories. Because it is understood that there are times when knowledge of history is necessary for appropriate decisions to be made, the Receiver functions as the main advisor for government. The plot of the story is developed around the apprenticeship of Jonas, the newly appointed Receiver. As part of his learning process, Jonas receives memories from the aging Receiver. As Jonas collects these memories, he comes to differently understand himself and his community. He learns, for example, that while his father is called "Nurturer of Babies," he is also responsible for the euthanizing of children deemed abnormal or otherwise unacceptable. Through the transmission of memories such as those of past wars or of winter sleigh rides, Jonas learns that the present is better understood when it is interpreted in relation to the past.

In order to develop the structures for the Commonplace Book experience within the classroom inquiry, it was necessary for us to contravene the taboos against writing in school texts.

This proved to be more challenging than we thought it would be. Even after providing students with their own personal copies of *The Giver* that we had purchased, and giving them permission to write in them, students demonstrated considerable resistance. In order to help students to overcome this resistance, I showed them my copy of *The English Patient*, pointing out all the markings on the pages, the sticky notes, and the more extensive writing on the blank pages at the back of the book.

After the first reading of this novel was completed, the students spent one month working with Dolores on matters that were related to ideas and themes drawn from the text. They became particularly interested in the idea of "sameness" explored in the novel, and they tried to understand why diversity needed to be valued. They studied issues connected to eugenics and euthanasia, and they learned about different civil rights movements. Throughout this month of research, students were continually asked to consider how their reading of *The Giver* informed their thinking.

Because I was interested in developing the Commonplace Book as an interpretive pedagogical practice, I returned to the school one month later to re-read the novel with the students. As this re-reading unfolded, the students became interested in new insights they were developing into the plot and the characters. As well, they continued to remark on how curious it was to look at their earlier responses. During our re-reading of the first chapter, for example, the students became agitated. Michele described an incident that had slipped by without comment in the first reading—the "release" of a pilot who had made a navigational error:

> *Now I know what released means! When I first read it I thought when they said the pilot would be released that he would just lose his job. Now I know that it means he will be killed!*

As we continued our second reading I encouraged the students to use a different color pen or pencil to add new notes, to answer questions they had asked, to record new impressions of characters, and to offer new interpretations of events. My questioning, after each oral re-reading, did not so much focus on their impression of that particular reading as it did on their awareness of the space between the two readings. I was particularly interested in having students notice and explain how their perceptions had changed since the first reading. In our discussions, I noticed how what was studied between the two readings had influenced their understanding of the novel. Irene referred to a documentary film they had viewed:

> *When I first read this book, I thought that the idea of 'sameness' was pretty good. I mean, I didn't think that there was anything wrong with that idea. But when we saw the film about Mauritius I started to think that maybe sameness isn't so good.*

At the conclusion of the week of re-reading students were asked to draw from the major themes of the novel, and their one month of research in between the two readings of it, to support the writing of short essays exploring ethical problems: Should society accept the practice of euthanasia? Should all people have access to information? Should everyone be able to freely choose to raise his or her own children? Although the essays convinced me that the students had changed their perceptions and understandings of ethical matters presented during the period of reading, interpreting, and re-reading, I learned later that there were other insights, not so easily noticed. In a discussion with a group of four of the students several weeks after the novel study ended, Gina mentioned that because her family would be moving overseas, she might be asked to discard her copy of *The Giver* with other non-essentials. She did not support this idea:

*But I can't throw it away! It's so ... lived in! It's stuffed with all my notes
and all my writing in it. I want to keep it so that my mum can read this
book and see everything that I've written in it. And then I'd like her to
write in it too so that I can see what she's thinking. I mean, if she gets to
see what I'm thinking I want to know what she's thinking too. And then,
maybe I'll keep the book and give it to my children and they can read it.
It will be like a history!"*

Inquiry that does not achieve coordination of behavior is not
inquiry but simply wordplay. (Rorty, 1999, p. xxiii)

What can be said about the use of the Commonplace Book as a
way to engage with literary texts? Following Rorty, these practices announce a rejection of the essentialist idea that an unme-
diated and transcendent set of truths about the world exists. Students were not asked to represent knowledge that they could
locate in the novel but, instead, were asked to become critically
aware of their developing identifications with characters and relationships to plot. These practices suggest that engagement with
literary fiction is not merely a practice where one identifies with
characters, learns moral lessons, and broadens perceptions. While
these are possible effects, the use of the Commonplace Book
highlights how literary engagements can function as archival sites
for creative and critical interpretation. Included in this literary
archive are the contributions made by the author (represented by
the printed text), the remembered and currently lived experience
of the reader, other published and oral material related to the
text, and the interactions the reader has with the various contexts of reading. In the case of the group and school reading
presented earlier, these contexts include shared interpretive work
accomplished during and after multiple readings of the novel.

Such insights into the experience of shared reading and response are certainly not original. Literacy and reader-response theorists have detailed the complex ways literary engagement and response becomes complicit with the layered contexts of reading (e.g., Beach, 1993; Bleich, 1987; Fish, 1980; Meek, 1991; Rosenblatt, 1978). What the idea of the Commonplace Book and the pedagogical practices developed alongside it add to these conceptual insights is an elaboration of the way personal and collective learning emerges from the organization and structure of literary engagement. In particular, the Commonplace Book activities, as described in the reading experiences presented earlier, show that self/other, mind/body, personal/collective, fiction/non-fiction, literary/non-literary do not exist as tidy demarcated categories but, instead, exist ambiguously and fluidly in relationship with one another. Most significantly, these activities illuminate the processes by which humans experience a sense of personal identity and how these experiences are necessarily organized by remembered, currently lived, and imagined identifications and relationships. This formulation helps readers of literary fiction understand that while literary engagements are considered to be imaginary, they are not considered to be less influential than other experiences.

Again, this is not really news to readers, teachers, or researchers of literary engagement. What is generally missing from many accounts of literary engagement, however, is an explicit theorizing of those engagements as sites of learning. Specifically, there is a lack of clarity with regard to what an anti-essentialist account of literary engagement might suggest about learning and how teachers might think about organizing for learning in schools, with particular attention to learning organized by shared readings of literary fiction. To illuminate this last point, I would like to briefly outline how Commonplace Book activities make explicit and support the continued development of the relationships between language and literacy, and experiences of maintaining a sense of self.

The English Patient's Commonplace Book shows how human beings have developed cultural artifacts and practices that function to help develop and maintain a sense of self. The Commonplace Book is not merely a collecting place for bits and pieces of interesting information the English Patient has gathered. Because it is continually subjected to re-readings, and is read and discussed by others who are trying to come to know the English Patient, the Commonplace Book functions as an ever evolving cultural archive that requires ongoing interpretation. The portable Commonplace Book becomes a crucial artifact for the English Patient who has chosen a nomadic existence, assisting him with the needed and ongoing process of interpreting a historical, contemporary, and imagined identity.

The English Patient's development and use of the Commonplace Book helps illuminate how human identities are organized by memory, narratives, and cultural artifacts. Maintaining a coherent sense of self, paradoxically, is not so much a project of self attention but, rather, one of attending to the many relations on which an ongoing sense of self depends. A sense of self, then, emerges as much from what is imagined as it does from what is understood as "real."

The Commonplace Book, of course, is only one example of many forms of interpretation practice invented by human beings. Other examples include rituals associated with Christmas, Hanukkah, Thanksgiving, and birthdays, which create conditions whereby humans are able to collect various expressions of their experiences into events that are repeated, but never identical. Each time a ritual is celebrated, the persons involved are challenged to interpret familiar practices surrounding that ritual with new knowledge and understanding. As Bruner (1990) has explained, rituals are tied to cultural, family, and personal narratives that function both to help individuals identify themselves and to create identifications with others.

As a number of writers have explained, many world citizens are experiencing ruptures and increasing complexity in their daily lives (e.g., Said, 1993; Bhaba, 1990, Borgmann, 1992). Not only has there been considerable shifting of national borders, new communication and other electronic technologies have created conditions whereby persons develop more of their conscious experience within a larger matrix of relationships. The young adults and children I work with, for example, do not only identify with family and friends that they meet, face-to-face, but, as well, often develop a number of relations in cyberspace. Coupled to the identifications humans continue to have with television, music, and movie personalities, it is commonly believed that human beings have more opportunities to elaborate their intellectual abilities than they have in the past.

This, however, may not always be the case. The experiences of characters in *The Giver* suggest that access to immediate webs of relations does not guarantee complex or deep interpretive development among persons. Although all citizens of the community described in this novel have ample opportunity to meet with one another in family and other social groupings, and to participate in meaningful forms of community labor, missing is an understanding of how their current experience is historically conditioned. Because historical memory is only available to the Receiver of Memories, other citizens have little interpretive understanding of how and why they exist as a community. Deprived of history and fantasy, most characters in this novel are confined to life within the descriptive or functional modes of language and thought.

It is through twelve-year-old Jonas that readers are able to glimpse what is missing from this society. As apprentice to the elderly Receiver, Jonas is provided with historical images and narratives that begin to condition a deeper understanding of his culture's current situation. This knowledge is difficult because it forces an interpretive imperative (Britzman, 1998). In order to accommodate new knowledge Jonas must revise the webs of understanding that condition what he currently believes. As his cultural memory is developed, Jonas creates his own commonplace for interpretation, one that helps him not only to understand the past but, more importantly, to use this knowledge to interpret what currently exists for him, as well as what might exist in the future.

The importance of relating historical narratives to contemporary situations is not unknown to educators, particularly English teachers. It is acknowledged that one reason for studying literary fictions is to gain a deeper understanding of historical events, whether of one's own culture or of others. In recent decades, the field of reader-response theory, particularly those views which emerge from Rosenblatt's theories of literary engagement, have helped teachers of literature to understand the importance of the relationship developed among readers, texts, and contexts of reading (Appleyard, 1990; Beach, 2000; Bleich, 1978). In schooling contexts, readers have been encouraged to represent their identifications with characters and, as well, to demonstrate how these identifications sponsor personal associations. While these have been significant developments, particularly since they point to a more expansive view of what constitutes critical interpretation, in my view there has not been sufficient attention paid to understanding how the very act of reading becomes immersed in a complex set of cultural activities that participates in the ongoing conditioning of personal and cultural knowledge and understanding. While there has been considerable theoretical movement in this regard, particularly from the post-structuralists (e.g., Derrida, 1992; Foucault, 1972; Kristeva, 1984), the insights developed have been difficult to incorporate into schooling practices, largely because these are viewed as relativistic, a perspective that is generally not welcomed in schools.

Following descriptions of pragmatist philosophy made by Rorty (1989, 1999), I would like to suggest that the Commonplace Book practices described in this book are examples of what I call "purposeful pedagogy." Within this pragmatist view it is critical to abandon the belief that there is a necessary correspondence between representation and reality. As Rorty (1999) explains:

> Pragmatists ... do not believe that there is a way things really are. So they want to replace the appearance/reality distinction by [the distinction] between descriptions of the world and of ourselves, which are less useful, and those, which are more useful. When the question of "useful for what?" is pressed they have nothing to say except "useful to create a better future." (p. 27)

A pragmatist philosophic perspective does not exclude the readers' identifications with invented literary characters as a potential site for the production of useful knowledge. For the pragmatist, literary experience is not considered vicarious but, rather, is considered *another* experience that is represented with a particular language by a particular reader. Literary engagements then, are not less influential than other experiences, however they are differently conditioned.

My use of Commonplace Books is aligned with the pragmatist view that interpretive understanding is best developed in situations where complex forms of relations are supported and subjected to various forms of interpretation. The purpose for engaging with literary texts, marking responses, discussing responses with others, and representing them in new forms is not so much to illuminate features of the novel. Instead, the goal is to use features of the novel to create conditions where reader responses can become developed, collected, and interpreted.

A pragmatist understanding of literary engagement is supported by the work of Iser (1989, 1993) who has named interpretive practices associated with reader/literary text relations a "literary anthropology." With this phrase he suggests that while the reader will always have an interpretation of the text she or he is reading, the interpretation itself participates in the ongoing development of the reader's self identity. Linked to Bleich's (1978) concept of interpretive community, which describes the way individual responses to literature are inextricable from the interpersonal, intertextual experiences of reading, the idea of literary anthropology is organized by the belief that a relationship to a literary text can become a productive site for the continued interpretation of culture and the way culture is historically influenced. It is within these literary commonplaces that readers have opportunities to review past, present, and imagined interpretations of themselves, of others, and to contexts of experience.

Philosophical hermeneutics offers views of interpretation that can be used to further elaborate the idea of literary anthropology and the use of Commonplace Book practices. For Heidegger (1977) hermeneutic inquiry is not merely the exegesis of biblical, legal, or literary texts. Rather, it is the study of human experience. The key feature of philosophical hermeneutics is that events of human perception are understood to be sedimented with experience and must be interpreted historically and contextually. Gadamer (1976, 1990) expanded this view into a dialectical hermeneutics where understanding is described as the interpretation of relationships between persons and cultural artifacts.

When studied in relation to the reader and the act of reading, the literary text becomes such an artifact and, therefore, becomes significant to the interpretation of experience.

However, the relationships readers develop with literary fictions do not wholly constitute the interpretive project announced by literary anthropology or philosophical hermeneutics. As demonstrated in my earlier descriptions of the research with *The English Patient* and with *The Giver*, literary engagements can only exist alongside the reader's remembered and imagined experiences. In order to create critical awareness out of these literary events, some explicit interpretive process is required. In our shared reading of *The English Patient* described earlier, the interpretive process included the juxtaposition of insights presented through the novel's characters with experiences we were having as a group of readers with one another and through our associations outside of the context of the group. As the characters in the novel came to learn about one another and began to invent new understandings of self-identity through their collective practices, as readers we were mirroring this process. Through the intertwining of literary and face-to-face relations, insights emerged about our personal histories and about our pedagogical beliefs and practices.

The creating of insight, of course, is not limited to literary events. Every moment of human lived experience requires that what is already known becomes accommodated to new information and situations. And so, while philosophical hermeneutics can be understood as a specific academic enterprise, it must also be seen as the same interpretive process human beings use constantly. However, in order for these daily hermeneutic practices to become more fully developed, they need to be made both explicit and supported with historical and contextual understanding.

As suggested by David G. Smith (1991), hermeneutics might be best understood as the project of trying to make sense of the relationship between experiences of being human and practices of making and using knowledge. Hermeneutic inquiry seeks to illuminate the conditions that make particular experiences and interpretations of those experiences possible. As such, hermeneutic inquiry is not merely a report of how things work, or an inquiry into the socio-political architecture of these events but, rather, is the activity of engaging in creative interpretations that become useful to the interpreter and, possibly, to others.

Although I did not realize it at the time, as a child I created hermeneutic interpretations that emerged from my identifications with literary fictions. As the only child of immigrant parents who could not afford out-of-school childcare, I spent many hours alone at home. Because I could read and had access to books from the local library, I occupied much of my time developing relationships with literary characters and their situations. In so doing, I learned early in life that my experience could exceed the structures imposed by adults. Although I do not recall re-reading novels, I remember continuing to think about characters long after the act of reading was completed. Because this ruminating occurred over a period of weeks and months, I learned that what I believed to be true could change. Important to my insights was the realization that while my circumstances changed, the characters and their situations remained constant. With the print text as a pivot, I could become critically knowledgeable about my own evolution. Because I was aware of the way in which my literary engagements were assisting me with interpretations of my experience, one could say that I was practicing a form of hermeneutics that would become useful to me later in life.

Of course, what I was practicing was nothing new. As Iser (2000) explains, hermeneutics emerges from deeply inscribed Western interpretation practices that have been strongly influenced by the Judaic traditions of interpreting the Torah. These interpretation practices have held, as their primary aim, the inventing of a relationship between a holy text and the current lived experiences of the interpreter. As a "closed" canonical text (that is, no new texts are added), the Torah functions as an interesting and productive historical artifact.

Within the Judaic tradition, Midrashic interpretation practices have been developed that support my pedagogical interest in the Commonplace Book. Foundational to Midrashic interpretation is the explicit acknowledgment that there is a difference between the Torah and the world outside the Torah—a difference that can be bridged and mediated through ongoing interpretive work. As this work continues, it is understood that the experienced differences between the two worlds are both upheld and eliminated. From this perspective, the mystery of the text can never really be resolved but, instead, is continually interpreted in relation to new contexts.

One Midrashic interpretive device is the "mashal" which, as Iser (2000) explains, is similar to a fable or parable and is inserted between the canonical text and the interpreter's immediate outside-of-text situation. The mashal creates a bridge between the canonical text and lived experience. The performative structure of the mashal is quite specific, beginning with the recitation of the invented narrative, followed by a brief explication of the narrative's applications, concluding with a "prooftext"—a short passage from the Torah meant to confirm the interpretations given. These textual interpretation practices have assisted with the ongoing creation of Jewish cultures that do not depend upon fixed geographical locations.

One might argue that the English Patient's practice of keeping an annotated Commonplace Book, which he makes available to both himself and to others, is a similar identification practice. Burned beyond recognition and sequestered in an abandoned convent with a nurse and two other refugees of World War II, the English Patient uses his copy of *The Histories* as both a reminder of who he has been and as a point of interpretive departure for who he is becoming. By juxtaposing his experiences with those of Herodotus, the English Patient is able to notice his own development and, at the same time, generate insight into his situation.

What the English Patient experiences, however, is not easily reproduced in school settings. In non-school settings, the literary text is usually experienced as an "open" text where readers feel able to insert, while reading, their own experience and interpretation. However, as I have explained elsewhere (1996), literary texts used for public schooling purposes function differently from those that exist outside those contexts. In particular, those texts that are designated as "curriculum" in schools are generally treated as though they are closed texts.

In the past, this closed canonical status was aligned with practices of close reading, where the primary goal of literary engagement was to discover truths inherent in the text. Although these practices continue to be upheld in both secondary and post-secondary situations, the belief systems supporting such practices have been subjected to a wide and thorough critique (Fish, 1980; Iser, 1978; Rosenblatt, 1978). This challenge has had its effects on public schooling, with increased use of reader-response practices becoming commonplace. However, it is important to remember that the inclusion of new practices does not necessarily replace other practices or the belief systems that support those practices. In my research I have noticed that although students are asked to consider the literary text "open" when they respond personally, they are also asked to consider it "closed" when they are asked to identify, with certainty, the main conflict, or the protagonist's tragic flaw. What can be done to make use of this tension in productive ways?

I suggest that the Commonplace Book practices used with children's reading and interpretations of *The Giver* represent the pragmatist belief that "truth" is identified as knowledge that helps to improve the quality of lived experiences. As an archive, the Commonplace Book can create the conditions for interesting interpretive sites where readers have an opportunity to develop an intertext that collects traces of various representations of their in- and out-of-text experiences. This intertext can exist as the relationship a reader develops through one reading of a text, an argument that Rosenblatt (1978) has made and which needs no further elaboration. I would suggest, however, that in order for the intertextual commonplace to become generative, practices of annotating, other forms of responding, and re-reading need to be engaged. As Iser (1975, 1978) has explained, the spaces of indeterminacy generated in the fictional text create the opportunity for generous interpretations. The commonplace practices I have described suggest that these productive indeterminacies be expanded through the addition of at least two sets of intertext annotations (in the form of in-text inscriptions) supported by individual and collective analysis. It is the practice of interpreting relationships among the in-text indeterminacies, *as well as* those created by several layers of intertext response that generates an interesting and productive interpretive site for readers.

Although such practices are not identical to the long and elaborate set of rituals associated with Midrashic interpretation, I do think that there are some parallels. Like Midrashic practices, the Commonplace Book practices used by the English Patient and those I used with elementary-school students reading *The Giver* required that readers continually invent a relationship—a narrative—that linked the world announced by the text and their remembered, current, and imagined worlds of out-of-text experiences. Further, in considering both *The Histories* and *The Giver* as canonical texts that condition multiple readings and interpretations, readers created sites where various forms of personal and collective interpretation could occur.

I use these Commonplace Book practices both with students in elementary and high school and with my undergraduate and graduate students. In most cases, students are able to use their annotations and their various intertext interpretations to generate insights they describe as important and helpful to them. In developing the Commonplace Book from their readings and re-readings of literary fictions, students create an interesting personal and cultural archive that requires interpreting. In providing them with structured reading and writing practices, I offer them an opportunity to piece together aspects of the canonical text, the narratives they develop from their relations with it, and applications of knowledge emerging from these relationships.

As a pragmatist, I would not try to discern whether students are "finding" or "making" truths from their involvement in these Commonplace Book practices. Instead, I would say that they are becoming involved in an exploration of how the process of developing relations with fictional characters and situations is creating a cultural archive that requires interpreting. I would also say that students are involved in a hermeneutic process. They are not merely trying to describe or explain the immediacy of their involvement with these texts. They are also trying to understand these involvements within the historical and textual contexts of their engagements. Most important, in creating and interpreting the Commonplace Books, students are generating insights that they find interesting and useful.

Earlier in this chapter I presented Gina's interpretations of her work with *The Giver*. In her statement, Gina wonders what would happen if she and her mother were to enter into a dialogue through practices of reading and annotating one copy of a novel. Generalizing from her experience of learning from her identifications with *The Giver* through re-reading practices, she speculates that she might develop insight into her relationship with her mother through similar practices. Perceptively, Gina insists that the results of this dialectic sponsored by shared literary engagement would be "like a history." With this phrasing, Gina is representing the idea that literary engagements are not identical to those she has with persons that she meets face to face. She is also demonstrating an understanding that these literary engagements have the potential to create experiences that participate in the ongoing project of making and using knowledge.

As places to work out relationships between familiar and unfamiliar ideas and experiences, Commonplace Book practices help develop conditions for the creating of insight. I believe that these practices represent a needed alternative to the now-pervasive belief that human civilization is more advanced because some of its citizens have access to seemingly unlimited sources of information. Information alone does not guarantee understanding. Information needs interpretation and the latter needs a learned method.

CHAPTER THREE

In this chapter, I offer an example of one product emerging from a Commonplace Book practice I used during and following research I conducted with a group of teachers from 1994 to 1997. This performance piece represents several intersecting circles of literary, theoretical, and interpersonal involvement. At the time of writing, I was thinking about recent experiences I had had on a weekend retreat on Vancouver Island. I was also re-reading Louise DeSalvo's (1997) book *Breathless: An Asthma Journal.* At the same time, I was continuing to interpret different aspects of my experience: my relationship with my family, particularly with my mother; relationships to books I was reading; relationships to new ideas that were emerging.

Although I claim to have kept a Commonplace Book, I did not keep one in exactly the same way as the English Patient. Like him, I inscribe books I am reading with a trace of my responses, and I choose to re-read favorite books in order to develop deeper insight into ideas I am developing. In the work that led to the writing of this chapter, however, my "commonplace" for interpretation was more ambiguously organized. Although it is not obvious from what is presented in "Troubling Bodies," the insights I am presenting were primarily influenced by my reading and re-reading of Hilton Al's (1997) novel *The Women.* However, by the time I encountered this novel I had completed my research with the teachers. It was in the midst of reading *The Women* that I was provoked to re-visit my research notes and to re-read theoretical and philosophical material related to issues that were represented in these notes. The "Troubling Bodies" writing, then, is not so much a report of research as a presentation of insight that eventually emerged from the juxtaposition of my engagements with a literary fiction, and memories and past representations of research and other personal experiences.

I call this writing "troubling bodies" since, for me, it represents how biological bodies, literary and theoretical bodies of knowledge, and cultural collective bodies continually intersect with one another. Although I suggest that these bodies can be "troubling" I also hint at the importance of making trouble. As I will elaborate in the next chapter, human perception needs to be interrupted in order for it to become better able to attend to the often-unnoticed details of daily life.

It is important for me to note here that what follows is not meant to be complete or necessarily self-explanatory. Although it resembles prose, I would urge readers to read it poetically. Like a poem, each section represents an image linked to an experience. Although the transitions between and among these images are at times ambiguous, the images are meant to be associated with one another. My aim in this piece of writing is to present readers with an interpretive challenge. Just as readers of poetry must do considerable inventing in order to evoke personal meaning from the reader-text relationship, this writing asks the reader to stitch together the stanzas with personal knowledge.

As mentioned in the Preface, this performance writing is connected to Chapters Four and Six. These chapters emerge from research contexts and attempt to show the researcher's and/or the teacher's complicity in literary and other inquiries. Together, these three chapters are meant to provide the reader with evidence of what can happen when people engage with literary texts, particularly when these engagements are supported by interpretation practices.

TROUBLING BODIES

April, 1996. Tofino, British Columbia. It is 3 a.m. and I can't sleep because my mother is having another night of asthma in the next room. She has joined my partner and me on our one-week retreat to a small cabin by the sea on Vancouver Island. Six months ago when I made plans for this trip I loved my mother and had forgotten she had this terrible disease. Now, as I lie awake for another night, I do not love her. She is interrupting our vacation. Even though I know better, I think this disease is her fault. Her body is troubling to me.

In her book *Breathless*, Louise DeSalvo (1997) interprets her personal experience with the sudden onset of chronic asthma. An accomplished Virginia Woolf scholar and biographer, DeSalvo uses her critical abilities to learn how her body has become troubling to her. She writes:

> When I work, I'm often oblivious to my body; it doesn't exist. This has all changed since I've been sick, and my body now makes me aware of itself with every stroke of my pen, every strike of the keys. I'm writing through my body in a way I haven't before. I wonder what this will mean? If my work will change? (p. 19)

May, 1997. Tofino, British Columbia. It is the middle of the night and I can't sleep because I am thinking about Terry's sex change. I have thought about this a great deal since Terry joined our Teacher Study Group last year. Tonight it becomes interesting to me that we are having our final retreat in the same place that we brought my mother last year. As I listen to the waves break in front of our cabin I realize I am angry with Terry. Why must she continually talk about her sex change experiences? She is preventing us from talking about the novels we are studying, from continuing the work I think we should be doing. But, then again, she is making our work more interesting. Her body is troubling to me.

In her review of the literature on trauma, DeSalvo suggests that diseases like asthma are likely, in part, the body's specific response to remembered traumas from childhood. Many asthmatics have reported chronic depression, substance abuse, anorexia, morbid obesity. They have also described a conflicted relationship with their body, often wishing it would disappear.

In *Phenomenology of Perception* (1962), Maurice Merleau-Ponty explains that humans are doubly-embodied. The fleshly body is, at once, a biological and a phenomenological structure. In recent years, Merleau-Ponty's theorizing about double embodiment has been confirmed by studies in neuroscience, which have shown that we are unable to enact experience without becoming biologically effected. Lived experience alters the brain, the nervous system, the immune system, the structure of DNA. It could be imagined, then, that the act of thinking might change what is genetically passed to children. Maybe there is a closer relationship between sex and knowledge than most of us have considered.

April, 1996. Tofino, British Columbia. During our time at the cabin, my mother continues her reading habit. She

CHAPTER THREE

only reads fiction, usually very long epic novels. She does not talk about her reading other than to say that she wonders what would become of her if she could not read. She always reads sitting up since asthma makes reading while lying down difficult. When she reads I notice her breathing improves, and there are long stretches with no coughing or wheezing. It may be that reading, literally, is saving her life.

May, 1997. Tofino, British Columbia. On the second day of our retreat Terry participates in a writing practice that asks her to make associations between our location by the sea and her past experience. Like others, she chooses to read some of her writing to the group, something that we have done many times before. Today she talks about her childhood, describing herself as a "puny asthmatic runt." Although she has mentioned this before, it is only today that this becomes significant to me. I think, perhaps, I am noticing this more now because as I look at Terry stretched out in her chair, she is anything but puny. She is Amazon, leggy, using a lot of space. Puny is not what I see. I realize that Terry is sitting in the same place that my mother sat last year when she was here, one eye cast to the horizon out the window. A shock of recognition occurs: Terry said she was asthmatic. My mind races to collect what else I remember from our past meetings: a distant father, a lonely childhood, a severe education, boys' schools where she was ridiculed. Plenty of trauma.

DeSalvo (1997) writes:

> I believe that asthma is a breathing disorder that is caused by abuse and that it is probably a manifestation of post-traumatic stress. I believe that asthma tells us that the person who has it is, or once was, so terrified that s/he feared s/he would die. (p. 147).... The body remembers. The body communicates. (p. 131)

Although reading *Breathless* convinces me that there is a relationship between the conditions that support my mother's chronic asthma and Terry's childhood asthma, I resist this knowledge, since it is easier to believe that the biological and phenomenological are not connected. But I know that my resistance cannot be defended. Not even by my own experience. And so I continue to try to understand. I am interested in what can be learned about learning by studying and interpreting DeSalvo's interpretation of her chronic illness, my mother's ways of living with hers, and Terry's decision to change her body.

I realize I have adopted my mother's penchant for reading. For as long as I can remember, literary relationships have been important to me. Recently, I have learned that these have also been important and interesting ways not only to learn new things, but also to increase one's capacity for learning. As DeSalvo and other literary workers such as Toni Morrison (1996) and Jeanette Winterson (1995) have suggested, involvement with literary forms creates necessary conditions for learning to perceive in more expansive ways. Literary relations are sites of interpretation. They are places where the work of art happens. And I mean this as the work of art *and* as the object of representation that this work creates. For me, literary engagements have interrupted what has become familiar in my non-literary experiences. The bodies of knowledge they have announced have been troubling to me.

DeSalvo argues that those who write, those who make works of art, are able to use these practices to create sites to interpret the relations between past traumatic experiences and current experiences. The work of art, then, is the work of critically interpreting the relationality that makes identity. It may be argued that Terry's sex change is a work of art. Making one's body the site of creation can become a place where critical interpretation is possible, not just for Terry, but also for those who know her. Working with Terry in our study group forced us all to reconsider what makes man and woman. We became troubled by what her body suggested about ours.

It is 5 years since the cabin experience with my mother and her asthma, 4 years since our retreat with our study group, 4 years since I first read DeSalvo's *Breathless*. When I first wrote this I was re-reading Hilton Als' (1997) book *The Women*, a strange genre that is all-at-once memoir, fiction, and theory. Most provocative to me is Als' theorizing of his identification with his mother, and of the complex ways in which her experience is continued in his. While all humans live out the historically conditioned past in their present, what strikes me as significant in Als' experience is that his mother understood her child's need to interpret these relations and, most important, that he needed interpretive conditions and tools. For her, this meant supplying him with fiction to read and notepads to write in. In creating art with words Hilton Als, like other literary workers, learned what DeSalvo (1997) suggests, "That works of art make the act of listening to the testimony of human suffering possible" (p. 78). And this includes one's own suffering.

Hilton Als and Louise DeSalvo write biography, literary criticism, and memoir. Terry studies biology and writes poetry. My mother reads fiction and studies asthma. I read theory and fiction and invent ways to think about reading. Curiously, all of us experience some relief from our symptoms when engaged in these works of artistic production and representation. The symptoms may or may not be asthma. There are other symptoms which, because they are less physically insistent, are more damaging.

The commonsense discourse of curriculum usually ignores the fact that we are, all-at-once, biological and phenomenological creatures. It does not believe, for example, that what is learned requires that our biological bodies adapt to that learning. It forgets that identity is relational, that it is mediated by biological bodies and by human made and other objects, including language. It mistakes the acquisition of knowledge for learning, rather than understanding that learning that matters to anyone emerges from the hard work of interpretation. It fails to remember that the work of art does not only involve the making of interesting representations of experience. As Suzanne Langer (1957) suggests, the work of art involves reformulating the already formulated, interrupting certainty, making trouble. For me, and for those artists with whom I engage, the work of art creates a gathering location for the usually unnoticed relationship between the biological and the phenomenological. Making a novel, a painting, a memoir, reading fiction, writing essays—all these create possible conditions where troubling bodies collect to engage in the necessary work of interpretation.

January, 1998. Tottenham, Ontario. It is Sunday evening and I am talking to my mother on the telephone. The miracle of this form of communication means that I can hear her congestion, although she tries to disguise it. I have learned that it is important for us to discuss what she is learning about asthma through her ongoing study of this disease. I share what I have heard about new therapies. She tells me she has made cabbage rolls for dinner. I tell her we are having chicken. She asks me about my work and I say something that I think she would construe as labor. I realize we are both familiar and strange to one another. She has a spell of coughing that lasts for a minute. She tells me she must hang up. I know she will soon be reading. I know I will soon be writing.

Learning How To Be a Subject

CHAPTER FOUR

In Mem Fox's (1985) picture book, *Wilfrid Gordon McDonald Partridge*, 4-year-old Wilfrid learns that his friend, 96-year-old Miss Nancy, has lost her memory. Because Wilfrid does not understand what this means, he asks his parents and a few of the residents at the "old people's home" where Miss Nancy resides about memory. They tell him different things: One person suggests that memory is something that is warm; another thinks it is something from long ago; two others believe it is something that makes you laugh or cry; another resident believes it is as precious as gold.

This research helps Wilfrid understand that having a memory is important, making him concerned that Miss Nancy seems to have lost hers. He decides to help her by collecting things that are meaningful to him: a box of sea shells, a puppet, a medal given to him by his grandfather, a football, a warm fresh egg. He brings these objects to Miss Nancy and, one by one, hands them to her. As they examine them, Miss Nancy begins to remember: She remembers the blue speckled bird's eggs she found when she was a young girl in her aunt's garden. She remembers a visit to the beach. She recalls, with sadness, a big brother who went to war and never returned. It seems that Miss Nancy's memory has been found.

In presenting Miss Nancy with objects around which she might narrate stories, Wilfrid demonstrates a theory of identity that calls into question commonsense views about what constitutes the experience of having a sense of self. Historically represented by Descartes' famous maxim "Cogito ergo sum" ("I think, therefore, I am"), human subjects have been led to believe that identities are lodged deep inside of themselves, beginning as some grains of predisposition present at birth, and are elaborated through social processes and with practices of learning. Common platitudes such as "find the real you" or "be all that you can be" or "develop your true self" demonstrate how this belief about identity has become lodged into the language used to describe what it means to be a successful human being.

But human beings do not experiences their selves as essentializations. Identity never really exists in ways expressed by commonsense discourses but, instead, occurs when memory intersects with projected contexts. I can never really pin down my identity "in this moment" since "this moment" is being used to interpret a relationship between the remembered past and the predicted future. That, of course, is why losing one's memory inhibits relationality and dramatically erodes one's experience of identity. In Miss Nancy's case, the loss of memory detaches her from the social world.

Although the author does not elaborate, it is likely that others before Wilfrid have tried to help with Miss Nancy's memory-retrieving processes. Perhaps family and friends attempted to stimulate Miss Nancy's memory by reminding her of incidents from their shared histories. Perhaps they even brought familiar objects to assist in this process. It is possible that they sang familiar songs to her, or recited favorite poems or passages from other favorite texts. But if they did these things, they were not successful. Only Wilfrid was able to help Miss Nancy become reunited with her past. What conditions was he able to create that others were not?

It is important to note that prior to the loss of Miss Nancy's memory, she and Wilfrid were friends. Unlike relationships people have with relatives who they often have known over a lifetime, friendships are more deliberately created. In order for Miss Nancy and Wilfrid to learn about one another, they likely needed to tell stories of their different histories and, importantly, they needed to share activities or interests.

I find it particularly interesting and significant that when challenged to help Miss Nancy with her memory, Wilfrid did not bring objects of *hers* but, instead, brought objects of his own. This strikes me as a rather clever strategy since it is likely that in the relationship of someone as old as Nancy with someone as young as Wilfrid, considerable time was spent examining things that one or the other person has owned. Even if it is the case that Miss Nancy has never seen the objects that Wilfrid has selected (and, this seems to be the case from the information given), she has likely participated in similar events of "show and tell" in the past. We are told, in fact, that Miss Nancy is Wilfrid's "favorite person" and that he "told her all his secrets." In asking Miss Nancy to examine the objects he has brought, Wilfrid invites her into a familiar narrative structure.

This strategy, it is worth noting, is supported by recent neuroscientific research, which has shown that the act of remembering something is much more likely to occur if it is contained within a familiar narrative organization (Calvin, 1996; Damasio, 1994). Similar to the way in which the words to a song are more likely remembered if the melody is sung than if the words are merely recited, the details of memory are more likely to present themselves within an event that previously has been associated with those memories.

This brief description and analysis of one event of remembering suggests what many before me have convincingly argued: identities are not discovered or found or predestined, they are made (Foucault, 1988; Kerby, 1991; Taylor, 1989). The making of identities is primarily associated with the ways humans have learned to use language to develop relations both with one another and, to some degree, with what Abram (1996) calls the "more-than-human world." From this perspective, one could say that Miss Nancy did not actually lose her memory. Rather, she lost track of the narratives that connected her present experience with her memories of the past.

In important ways, thinking about how one arrives at a sense of personal identity is necessary for thinking about how humans learn anything. After all, the most significant event that takes place in one's life is learning about one's place in the social, cultural and ecological order of things. This, of course, requires that one be able to identify and be identified as a specific "someone"—a process that involves processes of identification and differentiation. I am, in part, identified as "this person" because I am, to myself and to others, noticeably distinct from "that person."

It seems I am also able to keep track of my continuing identity by surrounding myself with particular objects, persons, contexts, practices, and narratives that describe all of these. My sense of self depends upon my current, remembered, and imagined relations. Some of these relationships are with people and some with other species (such as my dogs and cats). Other relationships are with characters that are made known to me through the novels and memoirs I read, and television shows and movies I watch.

That my sense of self-identity emerges from remembered and currently lived relationships with persons and with objects of the world helps me to understand why Miss Nancy might lose her memory. Not only is she removed from the familiar contexts of her past (her home, her neighborhood), but also she is likely removed from the daily living practices that would connect her to her own familial and cultural history. Without these daily contacts the sense of self that is organized by these overlapping discursive and dialogic structures can begin to dissipate. It can be argued that Miss Nancy has not really lost her "memory." What she has really lost is the story of who she has been.

I believe this is one reason why the elderly are often terrified of moving away from their homes into senior citizens' complexes. Without daily contact with cherished objects that are organized in familiar ways in known places, the topography of memory becomes interrupted. Moving favorite objects from the family home to the new situation doesn't help much since, of course, it is not only the objects of memory that matter, it is the way in which they are placed in space and time. The photos of the children that were hung in the hallway between the bedrooms and the main bathroom had significance, in part, because they were on the same wall that the children ran their mucky hands, or drew with crayons, or had their yearly height marked in pencil. The markers of memory are not lodged within the objects themselves but, rather, in the way these objects exist topographically.

During the final weeks of her terminal illness, for example, my mother continually worried that in the process of renovating her home for what we had hoped would be her convalescence, we might be rearranging things. "Don't move anything!" she insisted. "I want things to stay exactly as they are. I don't want you to lose anything." While we were concerned that the hundreds of books in her bedroom were collecting dust and, probably, affecting her health, we also understood that each of these books, placed in their specific place, were important topographical historical markers of her experiences. When she eventually agreed to have them moved out of the bedroom into new bookshelves we had assembled in the front room, she continued to worry that we had thrown the books away, until we brought photographs to show that they still existed in her home.

Of course, maintaining a familiar experiential topography is important not only to the elderly. As I prepared to work on this book I was terrified that I would not be able to begin, since my familiar working spaces were interrupted by a difficult move across the country. How could I think away from my office, my reading couch by the window? In order to begin, I needed to create a place for thinking that was as familiar as possible. And so, my partner and I painted the inside of our house the same color as the last house. I chose a room for my office that faced north, like my other office. I placed my desk under the window. I postponed buying the new computer promised by our new institution. I organized my files and my desk in ways that were familiar to me. I began writing by reading favorite works of fiction and memoir and theory. I refused anything new, stubbornly trying to recreate the landscape of my earlier thinking.

Once the walls were painted and the boxes were unpacked, I instituted my familiar writing rituals. As I think about these rituals, I am aware that these in themselves have become narrative structures that not only organize my work but also, in significant ways, organize who I believe myself to be. So that I do not "lose" my sense of self I need to maintain these practices, and I need to be able to find a vocabulary to describe them to myself and to others.

Knowing how identities are made helps illuminate how they are unmade. I remember, for example, why separating the adolescent students I taught in my early years as a public school teacher was sometimes successful. Although I resisted doing this, there were times when certain students needed to be segregated from the rest of the classroom group, usually because their behaviors had become disruptive. In severe cases, these students were given in-school suspensions. This meant that they were isolated in a single room with required work to be accomplished without the benefit of the usual forms of school sociality. Although this system was developed to prevent classroom disruption while maintaining a secure place for the student being disciplined, I can see now that this strategy was successful because it created a situation where the student began to have her or his sense of identity interrupted. Without the ability to associate, to exchange narratives, and to notice how he or she was affecting and being affected by the classroom and school culture, the isolated student began to feel insecure about her or his own place in the world. Upon re-entering the classroom, most of these students, while demonstrating the bravado typical of renegades who must show their peers they have been unaffected by these sorts of disciplinary measures, also presented a more tentative persona.

Many teenagers with whom I have worked have presented a strongly "fixed" sense of self that is based on what I have considered to be rather small amounts of experience and sets of interpersonal relationships. Sometimes this unyielding and inflexible self-narrative emerges from family situations that are tightly organized by fundamentalist beliefs, and sometimes it emerges from peer relations that are narrowly defined by qualities considered necessary to participate in that particular group. Although families are important to the early and continued development of personal identity, Harris (1998) has convincingly shown that more influential are the identifications children have with their age-mates, particularly within the context of school.

Attending school in large urban settings is no guarantee that the narrative of what it means to be a normal adolescent is any larger or more generous. Regardless of the size or the population of the school community, narratives specific to adolescent cliques within schools, and within groups loosely associated with schools, continue to narrowly define for the individual adolescent the codes of conduct and the ways of interpreting one's sense of self. Being aware of this information can help teachers understand why they are often frustrated in their attempts to change student behavior, particularly when verbal reprimands exist outside the boundaries of meaningful activities.

During my years as a junior high school teacher, I learned that by reading fiction with my students I could create a context for intergenerational interpretive work that was supported by the school curriculum. Although some of my colleagues considered this activity a waste of instructional time (they preferred to assign chapters as silent reading for homework), I learned early in my teaching that these shared oral readings created important pedagogical opportunities. By thinking out loud with students about my responses to particular characters and situations in the novels I read to them, I invited them to participate with me in the development of ideas. As opposed to much of their school experience that only presented ideas that were, apparently, already fixed and certain, these shared reading activities demonstrated that ideas and identities are always in process.

That shared reading of literary fiction should alter personal and collective perceptions and interpretations is not news. Reader-response theorists and literary critics have clearly shown this to be the case (e.g., Beach & Myers, 2001; Doll, 2000; Iser, 1978; Mackey, 1998). However, what is striking to me is the way in which these shared practices of reading can assist those with fixed identity narratives to engage in the needed boundary crossing that creates possibilities for the revision of these personal narratives.

Although Wilfrid Gordon can only know this intuitively, and not explicitly, I believe it is this sort of understanding that prompts him to collect artifacts to bring to Miss Nancy. As she examines them, and notices a relationship between an object and a memory, she is able to pull the thread and begin to tell Wilfrid some of her stories. However, one might wonder if these stories are an accurate representation of her biography. Or, is Miss Nancy inventing stories to replace those she can no longer locate in memory?

From my years of research into literary engagement it has become clear to me that the lines drawn between what are considered "truth" and "fiction" become largely obscured during processes of making and interpreting information, particularly when this information is represented as knowledge about one's own identity. For example, I cannot say with any accuracy which parts of my perceived sense of self have been developed by events that actually happened to me in my face-to-face encounters with humans and which have emerged from my identifications with fictional characters. I cannot say how I am affected by sensations which I have experienced, but which have not entered conscious awareness. I cannot say, for certain, how information I have deliberately invented about myself (fibs I have told about my experience to others) have become incorporated into the way I identify myself and others identify me. While commonsense theories of identity insist that my self emerges from my inherited predispositions as elaborated by my contacts with the social and cultural worlds, I know that this theory of self cannot really be defended. Whether Miss Nancy's "memory narrative" is an accurate representation of her history or largely an invention is not that important. What matters is not so much whether her memory narratives are true but, rather, whether they are *useful*. If these narratives help her to make contact with other people, in meaningful ways, and if these narratives assist Miss Nancy with the ongoing project of having an identity which she *experiences* as coherent and adaptive, then I would argue that they are doing the work that they need to do.

As a teacher educator, I have noticed that my students are preoccupied with trying to pin down what constitutes good teaching and good teachers. My telling them that good teachers have some passion for what they are teaching does not seem to help much. It's easier for them to think that good teaching emerges from strong management skills or from an unconditional love of students. Rather than trying to convince them otherwise, I begin most of my courses by helping them to make explicit the complex ways we humans learn to have a sense of self-identity and how the specific narratives that emerge from our experiences, in large measure, influence these identities.

I usually begin these inquiries by asking students to write autobiographical narratives of learning experiences they have had. While most students find this work interesting, they do not find it easy. Many aren't sure how to begin: "There is so much to write about!" they complain. Because experiences are complex, it is difficult to decide which words to use to account for them. Choosing to write about some aspects of one's experiences means deliberately excluding others.

That is one reason writers of autobiography find this work difficult (DeSalvo, 1996; Grosskurth, 1999; Salvio, 1999). It is easier to write about other people than it is to write about ourselves. As Fulford (1999) explains, it is impossible to know as many details about other people's experiences as we know about our own. That is why gossip is so fascinating for its perpetrators and so troubling for its victims. While gossipers revel in their ability to create a story from the smallest bits of information, those represented can only experience those stories as fabrications. And of course, it is why the victims of gossip are anxious to announce details of their experiences that are not represented by rumours: "That's not really the way it happened! What so and so failed to mention was that, while I did, in fact, give him a piece of my mind, I only did so in response to what he said to me!"

What is informally known as gossip, then, is not really the representation of experiences but, rather, is a bare-bones narrative, deliberately shaped and crafted, only loosely connected to something that has happened. However, since this narrative has sharp edges and a definite shape (or plot, we might say), it carries a certain authority because of its ability to be easily remembered and retold.

The fullness of our own remembered experiences, however, is not so easily contained within these structures. This becomes evident any time we try to represent an event that matters to us, whether it is providing a summary of a movie or trying to describe a traffic accident. As we make decisions about which details to include, we continue to be aware of all the fragments of information that did not make it into our narrative. Floating in and around our story, then, are the bits we remember, but did not include (Grumet, 1988). What counts as the text of our narrative only seems "truthful" once we have forgotten about what has been eliminated. I believe that this is one of the reasons that many people have a more positive relationship with their parents years after they have left home. In addition to the fact that adult offspring can begin to see parents as peers, it is also the case that the passing of time facilitates the creation of revised narratives of past events that make present relations smoother.

A number of scholars have suggested that what distinguishes the human species from other animal species is the learned ability to stitch together communal relationships through language use (e.g., Abram, 1996; Capra, 1996; Lakoff & Johnson, 1999). In addition to this connecting work, human language also functions to make sense of itself. And so, while we are engaged in the activities of using language to create relations among other people and other objects of the world, we are also using language to interpret and analyze our use of language (Harste, Woodward, & Burke, 1984). Furthermore, as members of a species that has invented various ways to represent language, we have extended what counts as the human mind. In my own daily life, for example, I rely heavily on information that is made available to me from printed texts, from the memory of my computer hard drive, and from the Internet.

As Foucault (1988) has shown, these language and literacy practices have become technologies of the self. This use of "technology" does not narrowly refer to machine technologies like the printing press or to electronic technologies like computers but, rather, refers more broadly to any set of cultural practices and processes that function to shape human consciousness. The use of gossip, for example, as a way for human beings to elaborate and shape relational identifications within communities is one sort of technology. Electronic tools, such as e-mail and web-based chat lines, have greatly enlarged and complicated the ways in which gossip-like communication practices shape experience. Another more widely experienced technology is the nightly news, which contributes strongly to an understanding of what constitutes noteworthy world events. While the nightly news is considered by many to be more authoritative than Internet chat lines, it is important to realize that both are developed through similar practices of discarding large amounts of detail in order to shape a small story of experience that is easily conveyed.

Disconcerting for 21st century humans is that while most of us have internalized the commonsense belief that we are primarily responsible for creating our own identities, we are reminded daily that this is largely not the case. Each time we hear of circulating gossip about ourselves, or read an evaluation of our performance written by someone else, or listen to a parent's version of some event from our childhood we become aware that who we think we are is largely influenced by experiences and narratives of experiences we do not control.

This is why I believe it is important that students in my teacher education class write small autobiographies of learning experiences they have had. Not only does this activity help them to understand that experience is much more complex than any language that can be used to represent it, but, as well, it gives them an opportunity to deliberately and explicitly create stories that function as one of the technologies that shape their own experience of self identity. Of course, writing these narratives is more than just an act of representing their identities. It is a productive act of creating them.

A few years ago, one of my students asked me what would happen if he "invented" experiences that had not really happened to him and represented these as actual events from his life. My response surprised him. "How would I know?" I asked. What is important to the autobiographical story is not so much that it accurately represent what really happened, but that it provide a reasonable account of what the writer remembers of what happened—or, if details of the event are fuzzy, *how* the writer remembers and interprets the event.

By asking my students to write autobiographies, I am presenting them with an opportunity to render explicit what is so familiar that it is often unnoticed. Because we simply cannot consciously perceive or remember all of the contextual details of events from our past, we continually engage in a process of re-creating images and narratives that give shape to what we consider to be our pasts. This is why it is impossible for anyone to remember a particular event from one's past in exactly the same way. Each time an event is remembered it must be interpreted within the current situation of recollection. As this recollection occurs, some coherence must be made between the most recent interpreted recollection and previous recollections.

These ongoing acts of interpretation are what permit human beings to continue to create coherent personal and collective identities in the face of ongoing contextual changes. As Flax (1990) has argued it is the *inability* to continue to revise narratives of past experience that results in various forms of neuroses or psychoses. In order for the human subject to continue to maintain relations with others in healthy and productive ways, she or he must continually reinterpret memories of the past in order to accommodate new contexts that shape understanding.

This is why I caution my students to be careful about how they choose to represent their autobiographies. Whether the narrative of one's past is a representation of a remembered event or an invented event, it is influential to the continuing development of one's subjectivity. When I use the term subjectivity here, I am not using it as a synonym for identity. While I understand an identity as something that has a particular represented shape that can be identified by one's self and by others, subjectivity is more an awareness of what it is like to have an identity. Subjectivity is the experience of knowing that I am a subject to my world and, at the same time, that I participate as a subject of other people's worlds.

Writing an autobiography, then, is a deliberate act of "changing the subject." It is a participation in a narrative technology that forces particular selections and arrangements of experience to be made. As the writer engages in these literacy practices, she or he begins to influence both the story that she tells about herself and the story that other people discern and interpret. Human identities, it seems, are continually invented — not found, not preordained.

This does not mean that I think one's sense of self is not influenced by biology, or ideology, or physiology, or environment. In fact, the belief that identities are invented emerges from a decidedly ecological sensibility. Like all animal species, human beings are intricately woven into webs of biology and geography. The sounds human beings eventually understood as "language" probably had their origins as imitations of and responses to other-than-human sounds: those of other species, of wind, of water (Abram, 1996).

The creations and ongoing refinements to written forms of language have contributed to accelerated evolution of humans and their capacities over the past several millennia. According to recent studies in evolutionary biology and in neuroscience (Brockman, 1995; Lewin, 1993), this has not only meant that language use has changed social and cultural structures, but that it has profoundly affected the ways in which the human brain and nervous systems are structured. As is now well documented (Calvin, 1996; Damasio, 1994; Pinker, 1997), learning and using language contributes to the early development of the human brain, particularly the ways in which neurons and neuronal clusters come to be more densely packed and richly intertwined in particular regions.

All experience, including the experience of learning, making, and using language is subtly marked on the biological body. This helps us to understand why the "nature-nurture" debates are too simplistic. Our brains are not biologically pregiven, nor are they created by our contexts and experiences. Instead, any act of learning affects brain structure so that a *different brain* participates in the next event (Deacon, 1997; Dowling, 1998). At the same time, each "new brain" carries with it its history of prior experience and interaction. The genetic constitution of the human species carries with it its own evolutionary history (Johnson, 1997; Maturana & Varela, 1987). While certain human genes are routinely expressed in each new human organism, a huge amount of "junk DNA" continues to be retained—vestiges of biological traits that have become obsolete (for example, webbed feet, tail, hair on body). It seems that just as words are sedimented with histories of their prior use and associations, so too is our genetic code woven through with usually silent possibilities.

Ecological studies are also clearly showing that one's involvement with context is never benign (Capra, 1996; Clark, 1996; Thompson, 1996). While it is obvious that human beings influence the environments in which they live, it is also the case that environment marks human biology and physiology (Abram, 1996; Lewontin, 2000). Of recent and growing concern, for example, are the effects of nuclear radiation and chemical pollutants. Now past levels where they can be readily 'absorbed' by the dynamic planet, these sorts of events serve to remind us that even very subtle changes in environment participate in the development and evolution of the human organism.

Discussions of the influence of one's involvement in ecological systems cannot ignore the fact that all components of these systems act and are acted upon. This means that ecological studies are not only concerned with the objects that comprise such systems but, as well, they are interested in their interrelationships. For persons interested in studying processes of learning and teaching, for instance, this has meant thinking about how the very acts of using language contribute to the ongoing biological development and evolution of an organism. As recent studies mapping the human cerebral cortex have shown (Kotulak, 1996; Norretranders, 1998), language use and literacy practices change the ways in which blood flows to different regions of the brain. More obviously, these acts alter the relationships that subsystems of the human body have with one another.

These insights have helped me to understand why it is important to have certain environmental conditions in place when I want to be productive in my academic writing. Because my work as a writer has emerged alongside my use of a computer word processor, I find that I simply cannot be creatively productive without the presence of a keyboard and a monitor. In my undergraduate days written work was wholly accomplished with pen and paper (typewriters were only used to transcribe the final draft), but my current work is never produced in this way. Now, I use my computer to incorporate brief written jottings I have made while reading into my creative work. I also require a window so that I can watch blue jays tease the squirrels. And some books piled on my desk to support my thinking. And a dog curled up on the floor under my desk that regularly reminds me that this writing is not the world, but only a small part of the world.

Like all human beings, I need some objects, some narrative tools, and a continually updated vocabulary to maintain a coherent sense of self-identity. I also need some creative projects. My interest in literary engagement has been supported by my decision to pursue a career that requires me to write about my insights. Like many persons who choose writing as an interpretation practice (Doll, 2000; Richardson, 1997), I have learned that writing is not merely a summarizing activity that occurs when all the thinking has been done. Instead, writing becomes a thinking practice in itself.

Of course, not everyone needs to use writing as a way to support thinking and interpretation. Some of my colleagues and students are mathematicians who use mathematical symbol systems and forms of representation to interpret phenomena and ideas. In so doing, they are not merely learning about mathematics, nor are they merely using mathematics to represent or symbolize a world. Instead, they are using mathematics to learn to perceive worlds of experience in ways that are new and interesting to them.

Other people develop different interpretation practices: gardening, quilting, cooking, making music or paintings, raising dogs or horses. Again, the practices, in *themselves* do not guarantee that interpretive insight is developed. Instead, these engagements merely become collecting places for the needed relationships humans require with other humans and with the more-than-human world in order to maintain a sense of self-identity. This is one of the reasons, I think, that Martha Stewart's television shows have attracted such a large audience. While most viewers will never collect antique linens, or cook exotic meals, or spend hours learning calligraphy, it is interesting to listen to people converse with Martha about their obsessions with these creative acts. Through vicarious involvement, viewers begin to notice that what is interesting about people is what they do that makes them interesting.

As my students and I interpret their autobiographies of learning experiences and read them alongside what we now know about the complexity of human learning, we begin to understand that good teaching is not simply a matter of incorporating good management skills, loving one's students, or being well organized. In fact, many of the narratives my students tell of profound learning demonstrate that many of these "rules" can be violated. What must be in place, however, is a particular understanding of the complex ways in which *what is learned* becomes woven into *who one is* and, as well, how one's personal biography is influential to how one interacts with new learning. The best teachers, then, seem to be those who have a committed interest in what they are teaching. At the same time, they understand that their personal interest, in itself, will not guarantee that students will be interested. While students are often initially attracted to the teacher's enthusiasm for particular subject matter, over time what is also needed are interpretive projects that help students to notice how new learning changes how they see themselves.

Such analysis helps us to understand that in bringing objects for Miss Nancy to examine, and by creating conditions for her to engage in a shared interpretive project, Wilfrid was creating the conditions for her to not merely *remember*, but to *invent* a new understanding of what is remembered. Unlike the "remembering" pedagogies likely imposed by Miss Nancy's family and medical practitioners, who were probably only interested in having Miss Nancy provide evidence that she could remember things *as she had previously remembered them*, Wilfrid is only concerned that he and Miss Nancy be able to continue their friendship through some shared interpretation project. In so doing, Wilfrid is able to create what my colleagues and I have called a "liberating constraint," a pedagogical structure that is specific, yet playfully open-ended (Davis, Sumara, & Luce-Kapler, 2000). It is within this interesting, specific, and playful interpretive structure that Miss Nancy is able to piece together fragments of memory around new objects of interest. She is able to do so within the familiar narrative structure of her already-established relationship with Wilfrid. This, I would suggest, is the most clever sort of pedagogy, since it admits that knowledge and human identities continually co-specify one another.

Importantly, the sort of pedagogy created by Wilfrid and the opportunities for my students to "invent" teaching identities through autobiographical work are both what I consider to be interesting forms of literary engagement. Although the tools and technologies of engagement are not the usual print fiction that I have discussed in other chapters, they are phenomenologically similar in that they require students to develop an identification with objects and narratives sponsored by those objects that are not usually encountered in daily life. For Miss Nancy, the objects are those provided by Wilfrid and the technology is the opportunity to create a "remembered" and interpreted narrative around these objects. For my pre-service teacher education students, the objects are their own memories of teaching that have been juxtaposed with the curriculum of teacher education, while the technologies include the creation of what Laidlaw (2001) calls "narrative tableaux"—written snapshots representing windows of memory that are interpreted.

In both cases, the interpretive acts remind participants that human identities are not predestined; they are not found; they are not discovered. Whether one is involved in creating gossip, or narrating past experiences, or identifying with literary characters, one is always in the process of inventing a new relationship among what is remembered, what is currently experienced, and what is imagined.

CHAPTER FOUR

CHAPTER FIVE

In this chapter, I offer a performative text that emerges from engagements I had with Anne Michaels' (1996) novel, *Fugitive Pieces*. These literary experiences were juxtaposed with historical, philosophical, and theoretical literatures concerned with interpreting relationships among history, memory, culture, geography, language, and identity. In addition to these textual artifacts, I examined personal objects to analyze how human identity is organized by cultural artifacts and, as well, how these develop new significance when understood in relation to emergent cultural knowledge (Morris, 2001).

So that my interpretations remain as richly textured as possible, a text that includes excerpts from, and interpretations of, literary fiction, autobiographical narrative, and theoretic and philosophic texts is presented. Following recent work by Alvermann and Hruby (2000) and Luce-Kapler (2000) I offer this text as an illustration of one way written texts might present insights emerging from research into human experience. Following this performative text, I present a review of influences that have helped me develop reader response methods and representation practices.

> "Write to save yourself," Athos said, "and some-
> day you'll write because you've been saved."
> (Michaels, p. 165)

In her acclaimed novel, *Fugitive Pieces*, Anne Michaels
(1996) interprets the tight weave of history and memory.
One character, Jakob Beer, a child survivor of the Holocaust, is smuggled out of Poland into Greece by archeologist Athos Roussos. On the small Greek island of
Zakynthos, Jakob transforms his sense of self as he
learns to remember in a new language. And he does so
again when, at the end of the war, he and Athos travel
to Toronto, Canada. With each change in geography,
Jakob must not only interpret his present circumstances,
but he must also accomplish a reinterpreting of his history. He eventually learns that history and memory are
not identical.

> History is amoral: events occurred. But memory
> is moral; what we consciously remember is what
> our conscience remembers. (Michaels, p. 138)

For Jakob, the relationship between history and
memory becomes central to his work as a poet. Like
many living in post-Holocaust times, Jakob puzzles over
the paradox of identity—an experience that announces,
at once, perceptions and images that are present and
those that are imagined. For Jakob, the historical and
imagined images are influenced by the traumatic memory
of witnessing the murder of his family. These remembered images continue to weave their way in and out of
Jakob's adult experiences.

CHAPTER FIVE

Jakob's caregiver, Athos, understands that while the traumatized body is inscribed by its own history, this history is never fixed. As they spend years together on Zakynthos and later, in Toronto, Athos tells geographical narratives of transformation. His thesis is profoundly simple: Just as geologic forms betray their histories, so too does the human body.

> The present, like a landscape, is only a small part of a mysterious narrative. A narrative of catastrophe and slow accumulation. Each life saved: genetic features to rise again in another generation. (Michaels, p. 48)

Athos finds 7-year-old Jakob hiding in a bog that was once the ancient timber city of Biskupin, now an archeological dig where Athos is conducting research. However, this research site would not continue for long. The Nazis eventually reburied the excavated city shortly after their occupation of Poland. It seems that in order to maintain their invented historical narrative of German superiority, any evidence of an advanced non-German culture was destroyed. And so, Biskupin's artifacts were smashed, the timber city buried. But not forgotten. It continues to exist in the archeological and poetic narratives that Jakob and Athos eventually write about their relations to this historical time and place. Each interpretation presents the way traumatic events become complexly connected to small, seemingly trivial events of daily life. As Michaels shows in her novel, the interpretive acts of the archeologist, the translator, and the poet are not meant to resolve history or to explain, in simple terms, the cultural present but, instead, exist to raise difficult questions about the relationship between history and memory.

> History and memory share events; that is, they share time and space. (Michaels, p. 138)

Every moment is two moments. Each speech act, each event (whether noticed or not) is the confluence of history and memory. Interpreting and theorizing any moment is another moment bearing the character of that which is remarked. Gadamer (1990) calls such activity the hermeneutic circle, referring to the way in which what is newly interpreted depends on what has already been interpreted as it simultaneously affects the ground of its own thinking and products. While we may say that there are two moments, history and memory, they exist as one and can only be captured, however imperfectly and incompletely, in what they contribute to the evolution of human thinking.

Since its publication in 1996, I have read *Fugitive Pieces* six times. As is my custom, I have penciled responses to each of my readings into the text. Like Ondaatje's (1992) main character in *The English Patient* I have created a Commonplace Book of my copy of *Fugitive Pieces*. As is true for many of my generation, particularly those of us who are children of immigrants, I feel compelled to interpret a relationship between my experience and the experiences of my parents. As I read Anne Michael's novel, and listen to her interviews, I realize that she is trying to do the same thing.

It is not surprising that those engaged in philosophical inquiry require literary identifications to create intellectual work (DeSalvo, 1996; Richardson, 1997; Salvio, 1995). Literary works of art are able to present conditions for thinking and interpretation that are not possible with books that are, written explicitly to communicate ideas, to make arguments. As Rorty (1989) suggests:

> [I]t is the disciplines which specialize in thick description of the private and idiosyncratic which are assigned [the] job of [associating theory with social hope]. In particular, novels and ethnographies which sensitize one to the pain of those who do not speak our language must do the job which demonstrations of a common nature were supposed to do. Solidarity has to be constructed out of little pieces, rather than found already waiting, in the form of an ur-language which all of us recognize when we hear it. (p. 94)

For me, the pleasures and problems of literary identification are necessary reminders that lived experiences are contingent upon the circumstances that organize such experiences. As I come to know Jakob Beer, for example, I understand that his ongoing development requires that he become adapted to new situations as they arise. These new situations are seldom predictable, but are always influential. Meeting Athos announces a new world of possibilities for Jakob: a new country, a new language, and a new set of opportunities. In changing languages and geographies, Jakob is forced to translate his understanding of his personal and ancestral pasts. Like the novelist herself, altered through the process of creating lives for characters to which she becomes attached, the characters of this novel are engaged in the ongoing work of inventing identities for themselves. It is the process of creating interpreted relationships among remembered, currently perceived, and imagined pieces that organizes the experience of self identity.

For Athos, continued reconciliation of the past with the present and the imagined future is performed in his work as an archeologist and historian. Work on his major book *Bearing False*

Witness, a critical history of Nazi destruction of historical sites and artifacts, functions as a practice that helps him interpret contradictory and temporally distinct facets of his lived experiences. Athos realizes that if Jakob is to also live interpretively, he must not only learn new vocabularies, he must also remember the vocabularies of his past:

> Athos didn't want me to forget. He made me review my Hebrew alphabet. He said the same thing every day: 'It is your future you are remembering.' (Michaels, p. 21)

Eventually, Jakob is able to understand his relationship to history, and to personal and cultural memory, through poetry writing. In continually challenging what Rorty (1989) has called his "final vocabulary" by inventing new ways of describing old ideas and images with poetry, Jakob is able to invent a more interesting subjectivity for himself and, at the same time, create new cultural artifacts that might help readers to do so.

This is also how I experience my engagements with literary fiction, particularly with those which have become favorites. My continued re-readings of *Fugitive Pieces* have been particularly productive, since I feel intellectually attuned to the characters of the novel and to the project of cultural and historical interpretation that these characters announce. While I have not communicated face-to-face with the author about her work, I feel that the two of us, through our shared relationship with characters she invented and with whom I identify, are doing some of the necessary cultural work of understanding what it means to live in post-Holocaust times. This literary commonplace continues to help me create a needed relationship between history and memory and, in particular, between the world of my generation and the world of my parents' generation. As well, it has illuminated, in productive ways, my nomadic disposition.

CHAPTER FIVE

PART II: LANGUAGE AND GEOGRAPHY

> Just as the earth invisibly prepares its cataclysms,
> so history is the gradual instant. (Michaels, p. 77)

In the last 20 years I have moved many times and have lived in four cities. I think I am getting good at moving, and yet, with each move I experience a sense of loss. Although I have learned how to negotiate new urban territories quickly, I do not feel that I have come to know them deeply.

> If you know one landscape well, you will look at all other landscapes differently. And if you learn to love one place, sometimes you can also learn to love another. (Michaels, p. 82)

Of course, place is more than geography. A sense of place includes the remembered and lived memories and narratives that organize human experience. When I speak of place, I am also speaking of human subjectivity. This is why I believe that my sense of loss with each impending move has less to do with leaving home again as it has with what leaving points to: a yearning for a vocabulary that might begin to give form to my personal and ancestral pasts.

The experience of being a subject is intimately connected to a lived and imagined language of family and cultural history. When I speak of human subjectivity I mean the way in which language, geography, history, and memory become collected into what can be identified as "I", "you," "us," "them." Learning to love a place means learning to love one's involvement in the historically weighted moment.

> The present, like a landscape, is only a small part
> of a mysterious narrative. A narrative of catastro-
> phe and slow accumulation. (Michaels, p. 48)

Even a nomadic person must find ways to invent an ongoing identity. Like many academics, I have organized my identity through relations with books and with persons I have come to know over the years. These relationships continue to thrive, and productive insights continue to emerge from them, because we read one another's work, communicate electronically, and, occasionally, meet at academic conferences. It is within and between these electronic, typographic, and physical encounters that I am able to maintain a particular thought over many months and years. In order to notice how my thinking continues to develop, I re-read my own work to remind myself of past relations to other people and their ideas. I also re-read my work to recall who I thought I was at the time of writing and to engage in the curious practice of wondering what has become of this person.

> The memories we elude catch up to us, overtake us
> like a shadow. A truth appears suddenly in the middle
> of a thought, a hair on a lens. (Michaels, p. 213)

This historical tracing of subjectivity through re-reading practices is not unlike my occasional wanderings through the small box of personal items I have carried with me through my many moves. In the past, these have consisted wholly of objects I saved which represent my own experience: photographs and letters, childhood treasures, the recorder that I learned to play in grade 4, evidence of achievements. Recently, I added my

CHAPTER FIVE

mother's collection of objects to mine: her report cards from the private school she attended in Germany before and during the Second World War; her marriage certificate (dated June 21, 1948) to my biological father; the land deed to the house she and my father bought in 1953; her collection of my elementary and high school report cards, clippings from newspapers; a German passport from my Polish father, dated 1940; a photograph of her at age 16 wearing the uniform of the Nazi Youth.

> It is a strange relationship we have with objects that belonged to the dead; in the knit of atoms, their touch is left behind. (Michaels, p. 265)

As I sort through my mother's artifacts I realize I am crossing a boundary into someone else's history. I examine documents that have been unfolded and folded hundreds of times over the years. A trace of scent creates folds of memory associated with handkerchiefs, deep coat pockets, and Saturday afternoons at Eaton's department store. This juxtaposition of my mother's and my own artifacts creates curious interpretive possibilities: What can be said of her age 16 picture and mine? Both clear-skinned, light-eyed, half-smiling faces that to another observer could be seen as brother and sister.

> We think of photographs as the captured past. But some photographs are like DNA. In them you can read your whole future. (Michaels, p. 252)

Maurice Merleau-Ponty (1962) reminds us that humans are both biological and phenomenological creatures. Human identities are organized by their physiologi-

Every Moment is Two Moments

cal structures and their cultural organizations. Recent studies in neuroscience (e.g., Deacon, 1997; Johnson, 1997) have confirmed that the human biological system is marked by experience. Research in complexity theory (e.g., Capra, 1996; Cohen & Stewart, 1994) has expanded this idea, showing how human bodies co-develop with geographic, meteorological, economic, political, and social systems. This knowledge has helped those of us interested in human science research to understand that our inquiries must never be solely confined to examining the personalities, the objects, the contexts or the histories of our worldly engagements. Such inquiries must also be interested in interpreting the relations among these things.

> On the map of history, perhaps the water stain is memory. (Michaels, p. 147)

As I study my newly expanded collection of artifacts I am provoked to wonder about their relations to one another and, especially, to the ways they announce questions about geography, memory, language, and identity. In particular, these objects ask me to develop a more fully interpreted understanding of my own relationship to my parents and to their contexts of experience, including their emigration from post-World War II Europe to Canada. What can I say about how those events and how interpretations of those events have participated in the creation of my own subjectivity?

> Never trust biographies. Too many events in a man's life are invisible. (Michaels, p. 141)

CHAPTER FIVE

In *A Chorus of Stones: The Private Life of War*, Susan Griffin (1992) layers autobiographical narratives and historical accounts of nuclear destruction with personalities and events associated with the Holocaust. Her thesis is that the usually unknown aspects of experience continue to be influential. Family secrets about alcoholism and incest, for example, color and shape personal identities and collective relations even if they are never disclosed. The unknown details of traumas such as the nuclear destruction of Hiroshima or the murder of millions of Jews during World War II continue to shape historical interpretation and memory.

As I read Griffin's interpretations, I realize that the gaps in my knowledge about my family are astonishing. I know only a small amount about my mother's family, almost nothing about my biological father's. Most of what I know of my mother's family has been gleaned from often-repeated small stories she told me over the years—stories that, as I explain later, do not offer more than an overview of only a few events.

I am not alone in my ignorance of family and cultural stories. A large number of Canadians and Americans of my generation trace their immediate ancestry to the events in Europe during and following the Second World War. Many of my childhood friends were the descendants of German, Polish, Dutch, Russian, and Italian parents. Although most of my friends' parents spoke their first language at home, mine did not. Largely because they did not share a common first language, the language of their marriage was English, a second language they learned together. But it was not the English that I know. It was less sure, shaped by German and Polish sensibilities and intonations. More than any other changes they made, for my parents the change of language required a radical alteration in subjectivity. As Gerda Lerner (1997) suggests:

> When you lose your language, you lose the sound, the rhythm, the forms of your unconscious. Deep memories, resonances, sounds of childhood come through the mother tongue—when these are missing the brain cuts off connections. (p. 39)

My mother left Germany in 1949, one year after her marriage to her first husband, a Polish soldier who was working in her family's village immediately following the Second World War. At that time, according to her account of it to me, it was not desirable for Germans to marry persons of other nationalities, and so emigration to another country for couples of mixed ethnicity was common. Despite my mother's post-secondary education and newly acquired status as a member of the educated middle-class in post-World War II Germany, she arrived with her new husband in Canada to work as a farm laborer. Her certificate from the "Displaced Persons Professional Testing Board" classified her as a "housemaid." My father is classified as both a "farm worker" and "wood worker."

My mother arrived in Canada with her work visa and some treasures from home, including a package of her favorite opera records. She also brought a love of literature, a strong education in the arts, and a desire to continue a life of intellectual stimulation she experienced during her education at the convent school. The latter remained largely unfulfilled. She worked as a housemaid for 3 years and then in dry cleaning establishments until her health failed in 1984.

> Language. The numb tongue attaches itself, orphan to any sound it can: it sticks, tongue to cold metal. Then, finally, many years later, tears painfully free. (Michaels, p. 95)

Of course, German continued to insert itself into the collective consciousness of our family. Even though the German language did not organize everyday domestic relations in our house, it was felt in the food prepared, in the opera records played, and in the songs sung. Eventually, however, even these slipped away. In the last 15 years meals were primarily inspired by recipes from magazines and music reflected popular North American tastes. Once retired, a great deal of my mother's time was taken up with the reading of romance and mystery novels. She continued to insist that she would die if she could not read. I believed her and that is why I knew she was dying when, one day at the hospital, she announced that she no longer found reading interesting.

> And later, when I began to write down the events of my childhood in a language foreign to their happening, it was a revelation. (Michaels, p. 101)

Language does not exist as a veil between subjects and objects but, rather, functions to connect and interpret the experiences that constitute one's experience of identity. The capacity to use language to create links among things that are present to consciousness, as well as to things that are remembered or predicted, gives humans a unique ability to interpret the relations of past, present, and projected experience. Supported by the capacity to remember, to bear witness, and to interpret history, humans are able to engage in the imaginative acts of reconsideration and creative invention.

In the last several decades work in curriculum theory (e.g., Pinar, Reynolds, Slattery, & Taubman, 1995), cultural studies (e.g., Grossberg, Nelson & Treichler, 1992) and interpretive research methods (e.g., Denzin & Lincoln, 1994) has revealed how discursive practices shape experiences and how they influence interpretations of experience. Borrowing from literary theory, pragmatist and continental philosophy, psychoanalysis, and post-structuralism, researchers of human experience have learned to pay attention to how people are involved in overlapping, shifting, and contradictory narratives. Rather than representing experience, discursive practices create experience.

As a first generation Canadian of parents who became exiled in English, I have found it challenging to piece together an identity that makes sense to me. Much of this difficulty, I have recently come to understand, emerges from my history of living with an older generation who forgot the resonances of early memories through the loss of their first language. While my parents found ways to represent their early experiences with English, it was evident to me that these were unsatisfying to them. As various scholars have suggested (e.g., Hoffman, 1989; Lerner, 1997), it is impossible to translate memories from one language to another.

> Athos's stories gradually veered me from my past. Night after night, his vivid hallucination dripped

> into my imagination, diluting memory. (Michaels, p. 28)

During the last weeks of her life, my mother becomes preoccupied with narrating events from her childhood and young adulthood in Germany. There is the story of how each Sunday her mother drove a bicycle 30 kilometers to the convent school to visit the Mother Superior. "That was her holiday," she tells me. "After working to keep the farm going for 6 days, on Sunday she came to have coffee with the Mother Superior. That was her holiday." She remembers the time black cars came and took the nuns away: "I never saw them again. They turned the school into a hospital." There is the story of my grandfather returning from the prisoner-of-war camp. My mother is the first to notice his approach, although she does not recognize him. "I saw him coming up the road. I called to your grandmother, 'Here comes another hungry one.' He was never the same."

> Sometimes the body experiences a revelation because it has abandoned every other possibility. (Michaels, p. 53)

I have come to believe that in the last part of her life my mother tried to represent her early experiences, but with the English language it was not possible to convey the depth of her knowledge. While continuing to be identified as a German woman because of her accented English, she had become disconnected from the German language and, as a result, from the resonances of her childhood. Her German experiences could not be adequately captured in English, no matter how many times they were told. As a native English speaker, I continued to be frustrated with the thinness of the narrative. I yearned for more nuanced and literary accounts of my mother's early years. I wanted to hear, in more emotionally charged ways, how she experienced the contradictions of living in Nazi Germany during the years of her adolescence.

> Truth grows gradually in us, like a musician who plays a piece again and again until suddenly he hears it for the first time. (Michaels, p. 251)

Days before her death, I show my mother a new book that I took part in authoring. It is a selfish act, since I understand that at this point in her life books do not matter. I point out personal photographs that my co-authors and I included in the book. One photograph is of my mother reading. "Do you recognize this person?" I ask hopefully. She peers at the picture and shuts the book. "It's an ugly old woman." I am startled by her response. She resumes leafing through the book, finding the pictures of the house she and my father built from materials discarded from the old Municipal Hospital. "That's my house. That's a picture of your father in the war." She closes the book and fixes her eyes on me: "How did I ever get such a smart son?" She does not mean this rhetorically. It is a real question, announcing the incredulity parents experience when they realize that they and their children have different stories, different songlines.

> After burying the books and the dishes, the silverware and photos, the Jews of the Zakynthos ghetto

> vanish. They slip into the hills, where they wait
> like coral; half flesh, half stone.... In their cramped
> hiding places, parents tell their children what they
> can, a hurriedly packed suitcase of family stories,
> the names of relatives. (Michaels, p. 40)

In his book *My German Question* Peter Gay (1998) interprets memories of living in Nazi Berlin from 1933 to 1939. In providing details of the conflicted ways he exists both inside and outside German history, language, and culture, he is able to show how identity is never stable or resolved. Like the characters in *Fugitive Pieces*, Gay continues to experience the curious ways the weight of the past endures in the present moment. While it is impossible to escape the effects of memory and history on consciousness, it is possible and necessary to interpret these effects. According to Gadamer (1990), this is an important project for humans who have developed language as a way to organize memory. Hermeneutically speaking, it is important to make sense of my parents' lives, not so much to understand them, but to understand how their experience continues in mine.

> The present, like a landscape, is only a small part
> of a mysterious narrative. (Michaels, p. 48)

In the end, I do not believe that my mother was able to say much more about her experience of growing up during the Second World War. Not only did a language that could not adequately represent her memories limit her, but also she was constrained by the interpretive tools that had been made available to her. Unlike myself, she did not have an opportunity to spend a large part of her life contemplating her own experience and learning how to critically interpret it. Instead, like many immigrants, she worked to connect the fragments of lives organized by two languages, two countries, and two cultural and social contexts.

I do not believe that she ever fully resolved her conflicted relationship to her own immigration, the loss of her parents and grandparents, or the loss of her language and nation. Before arriving in Canada to invent a new life, her subjectivity was overdetermined by cultural narratives about who immigrant women were generally, and who German women were, specifically. But, of course, her life does not end with the demise of her biological body. It continues to exist in the artifacts she left behind, in the memories of her family and friends, and in the narratives of hers that we have made ours. It exists, in significant ways, in this writing.

90

> I knew suddenly my mother was inside me. Moving along sinews, under my skin the way she used to move through the house at night, putting things away, putting things in order. (Michaels, p. 8)

My position as what Rorty (1989) has called a "liberal ironist" helps me to better understand the difficulty of being theoretically aligned with anti-essentialist discourses and, at the same time, being identified with the political left. I am committed to social justice and to eliminating the cruelties imposed on certain individuals and groups. I understand that language can never fully represent the complexity and fullness of human identity and experiences of identity. I also know that in order for individuals to experience a sense of personal and cultural coherence, language must be used to create identities that can be recognized. And so, while I do not want to essentialize human identities, I understand that to some extent categories are necessary heuristics. I also know, however, that any experience of identity is contingent. It emerges from a biological, geographical, social and cultural history that is given shape and form by language. This helps me to remember that my experience of identity is never really present to me but can only exist after the fact, in the memories and narratives that organize who I believe myself to be (and who I believe others to be).

As part of my personal project of reconciling contradictions and difficulties I experience, I engage in reading and writing interpretation practices. I do some of this work in order to critically understand the generation that preceded me. I do not do this to condemn or celebrate them. I do so because their experience continues in mine and, therefore, I am obligated to try to understand what this means. I experience this as a creative act of invention. I do not discover my identity. I participate with history and with contemporary culture in the making of it. Part of this ongoing process of invention is to learn to incorporate identifications with those who identify and are identified as historically other to me. And so, I continue to read books written by people whom I have not met but through whose work I identify. Some of these books are memoirs. Some are fictions. Some are works of philosophy or theory. I think about what it means to create these literary and theoretical commonplaces, using my current vocabulary to help me to interpret the relationship between my own sense of identity and my vocation—the practice of teaching and the researching of literary engagements.

However, reading and thinking do not complete the creative process. As Borgmann (1992) suggests, it is important to make something that can contribute to the interpreting of history and the creating of human subjectivity and culture. My work, as I have come to understand it, is to collect the fugitive pieces of history and memory—the bits and pieces of what I find in literary, historical, autobiographical, and other fictions—and stitch them together into interpretive essays that attempt to represent the evolution of an idea.

> One can look deeply for meaning or one can invent it. (Michaels, p. 136)

In her books, *Literature as Exploration* (1938) and *The Reader, The Text, The Poem* (1978), Rosenblatt argues that the reading of literary texts is an important and unique way to explore the human condition. Unlike some of her contemporaries who insisted that literary meaning could be extracted from a text or from an examination of the contextual and historical circumstances leading to the production of that text (e.g., Leavis, 1950 [1932]; Hirsch, 1976), Rosenblatt suggested it is the relationship between reader and text that structures the production of meaning. Concurring with literary reception theorists such as Todorov (1977) and Iser (1978), and following Dewey's (1996[1916]) pragmatist philosophy, Rosenblatt theorized the relationship between reader and text as a site for the production of knowledge, not merely the interpretation of knowledge. As is now commonly believed, readers do not extract knowledge from a text, nor do they impose personal knowledge on it. Rather, readers and texts and contexts of reading collaborate in the continued inventing and interpreting of knowledge.

These sites of production are not reserved for experiences that Rosenblatt describes as "efferent." For Rosenblatt, the efferent is related to the instrumentally communicative function of language, while the aesthetic emerges from the experience of being drawn into language that fulfills a formulative function. Lewis (2000) has convincingly argued that the sort of aesthetic experiences described by Rosenblatt must include an understanding of the complex ways readers' identifications with texts are social and political events, which create opportunities for the pleasures associated with the development of critical insight. From this perspective, literary engagements can be (and usually are) sites for both aesthetic enjoyment, and creative and critical learning.

This understanding of reader-response theory is compatible with constructivist theories of learning, which describe the learner as co-emergent and co-evolving with the knowledge that is produced (Spivey, 1997; von Glasersfeld, 1995). When a reader engages with a work of literature she or he does not merely experience the characters vicariously or learn moral lessons from their actions. As Beach (2000) has explained, the reader's involvement with text continues to represent the complex ways she or he is involved in various activity systems, such as book clubs or classrooms, which both shape and are shaped by literary relationships. And, as the developing field of enactivist learning theory is demonstrating, all of these cultural associations are continually influenced by both biological and ecological systems (Davis, Sumara, & Luce-Kapler, 2000; Varela, Thompson, & Rosch, 1991). Such overlapping relationships are made more complex by the human capacity to remember, represent, and reinterpret. During and following active involvement with the literary text, the reader reflects upon past, present and future experiences.

In recent decades, a number of anthropologists have written about the emerging relationship between anthropological inquiry and literary studies (e.g., Bateson, 1994; Behar, 1996; Geertz, 1988). Following post-structural theories that conceptualize language as a continually emergent system that is unable to completely represent the fullness of human experience (Derrida, 1976, 1978), these theorists have challenged the commonsense belief that researchers are able to represent, unambiguously and exactly, the experience of others. Their work has contributed to an increased interest in the relationship between knowledge and literacy representation practices.

Because most human science researchers depend on print text for the dissemination of their research, the question of authorship and the relationships between truth claims and the writing of text have been closely examined (Behar, 1996; Clifford & Marcus, 1986; Richardson, 1997). Over the years, this scrutiny has helped researchers to understand that while there continues to be an obligation to interpret culture, the reporting of this must be understood as a particular kind of fiction, where fiction is understood as the author's selection and interpretation of experienced events (Lather, 1991; van Maanen, 1988). Understanding research reports as forms of fictional representation has facilitated an understanding of ethnographic writing as an interpretive art that relies upon many literary conventions in representations of knowledge (Richardson, 1997).

As discussed briefly in Chapter Two, Iser (1989, 1993) has named interpretive practices associated with reader/text relations a "literary anthropology." With this phrase he suggests that while the reader will always have an interpretation of the text she or he is reading, the interpretation itself participates in the ongoing development of the reader's self identity. Linked to Bleich's (1978) concept of interpretive community, which describes the way that individual responses to literature are inextricable from the inter-personal, intertextual experiences of reading, literary anthropological research is organized by the belief that a relationship to a literary text can become an interesting location for the continued interpretation of culture and the way culture is, as Heidegger (1966) argues, historically weighted. It is within these literary commonplaces that readers collect past, present and projected interpretations of themselves and their situations.

The relationships developed with literary fictions, however, do not complete the interpretive project announced by the practice of literary anthropology. Literary relationships can only exist as information alongside other remembered and imagined experiences of the reader. In order to create critical awareness from these literary anthropological events, some explicit interpretive process is required. For example, in preparing the performative text presented earlier in this chapter, I spent several weeks re-reading and responding to my notes from previous readings of *Fugitive Pieces*, and making notes of non-literary works that I believed were topically related to matters of research interest.

The process of literary anthropological inquiry only begins with practices of juxtapositional reading and note taking. As explained in Chapter Two, these responses require interpretation if they are to become useful to the researcher and, eventually, to those who examine the researcher's published analyses. For me, this means that subjects of research interest must become known as complexly and deeply as possible. For example, in order to try to understand my relationship to my parents, I have spent years reading histories, memoirs, literary texts, and philosophical arguments written by those who are interested in matters connected to events of World War II, including the exodus of Germans from Europe after the war. As I read these texts, I always annotated them, and created binders of "booknotes" which contained favorite quotes and short interpretive response passages.

Because I concur with those who argue that literary texts (particularly novels) create strong reader identifications and opportunities for interpretation of the meanings generated (Iser, 1993; Eco, 1994; Grumet, 1988; Rorty, 1989), I begin processes of analysis by selecting one novel that functions as my "commonplace text." As I explained in Chapters Two and Three, usually this is a text I have read several times. As I complete each reading, I continue my practice of recording cryptic notes into margins and on any other white spaces available. As well, I record the date and conditions of my reading experiences on the inside front cover. Each time a reading is completed, I re-visit my booknotes for that novel, adding new quotes that I have found interesting and, as well, new interpretations that I create as I am typing these quotes.

When I re-visit a literary text I have previously annotated, I remember the context of my last reading(s) and, at the same time, notice how my current reading context has changed. In foregrounding the historical and contextual aspects of my interpretive situations and practices, and in creating information that represents these aspects, I am developing an archive of data that supports my research questions and interests.

At the same time, these textual annotating and re-reading practices help to foreground the way that language continues to interact with memory in the ongoing development of human identities. Although language is a human invention, it is seldom considered as such. Because it has become so intertwined into human societies, language has become the unnoticed backdrop of experience and, therefore, is no longer understood to be a cultural tool. As I re-visit literary texts I have read and annotated more than once, I am continually reminded of the complex and ever-evolving relationships among language, memory, forms of representation, and senses of personal and cultural identities.

As I suggested in Chapters Two and Three, insight often emerges when a literary text becomes the "commonplace" around which ideas are developed and interpreted. For me, and for those who have used this method with me, such reader-response practices help to organize ideas and other information without the reader becoming overwhelmed with trying to include too much detail in the interpretive report.

It is important to note that I select novels to function as commonplaces that offer what Iser (1978) describes as instances of indeterminacy. He describes indeterminacies as those gaps in understanding suggested by the text, which must be filled in by the reader. Although, of course, all literary texts contain indeterminacies, I aim to select texts that challenge me and/or the readers with whom I am working to expand our perceptions and interpretations. For example, in research with grade five and six elementary school students my colleagues and I (Sumara, Davis, & van der Wey, 1998) selected Lois Lowry's (1993) science fiction novel *The Giver.* Although most adult readers would likely consider this novel an easy-to-read example of science fiction, for the students it proved to contain many indeterminacies that required explicit interpretation. In my research with high school English teachers who were interested in learning about the relationship between their personal literary reading experiences and their teaching practices (Sumara, 1996), it was necessary to use a novel that departed from structures expected by avid readers of literature. In this research with teachers, Michael Ondaatje's (1992) complex novel *The English Patient* was necessary to create the desired effect. In the research described at the beginning of this chapter, the novel *Fugitive Pieces* was sufficiently unusual in its narrative structure to provoke me to read slowly, to re-read, and to elaborate productive interpretive sites from the indeterminacies provoked by my engagement with this text.

Literary anthropological reader-response methods are distinguished from all forms of literary criticism through an interest in interpreting and further developing what is *conditioned* by literary identifications and interpretations, rather than emphasizing the interpretations themselves. Although the reader's identifications with characters and plots are crucial to the development of insight, these only account for one part of the process. More crucial is the way ongoing re-readings of the texts create a form of mindfulness, similar to a meditative practice, where readers continue to collect new information and interpretations in the commonplace organized by their literary engagements. With each return to the literary text, the reader/researcher is compelled to interpret the gap that exists between this reading and the last one, thereby creating a generative recursive process.

Many people have asked me if this process is limited to print fiction. Can literary anthropological work be created through identifications and responses to other representational forms, such as memoirs, theoretical texts, or movies or television shows? Concurring with arguments made by Eco (1994), I believe that literary texts create generous locations for interpretive inquiry because of the way readers organize their perceptions with them. When readers engage with memoirs, for example, they believe that what is being presented is an account of something that actually has happened. The reader of memoir, then, agrees to believe that what the writer is reporting is "true," even if the reader understands this as a subjective truth. Novels, however, are another matter. In writing a novel, the author *pretends* to be telling the truth and the reader *pretends* to believe that what the author is writing is true. It is the experience of "pretending to believe" that creates the sort of open, playful interpretive space that allows readers to insert their own experiences and interpretations to account for perceived gaps in the narrative. While a reader might be reluctant to invent missing details in a memoir that is being read, she or he willingly invents details to overcome indeterminacies while reading a novel.

Of course, the experience of "pretending to believe" occurs whenever persons watch television comedies or dramas, or when viewing a movie, or when interacting with contacts on Internet chat lines. However, it is my contention that these experiences do not usually create the same depth of interpretive experience that can occur with repeated readings and interpretations of novels, largely because the encounters are fleeting, and usually not subject to re-visiting. This, however, does not mean that identifications with other kinds of imaginative forms do not have a contribution to make in the ongoing human quest to develop personal and cultural insights. In my teaching and research, I sometimes include the viewing and interpreting of movies with students and research collaborators. If the movies are structured with some challenging indeterminacies, and if there are opportunities, over time, to view the movie several times, and engage in juxtapositional reading and interpretation practices, these can create similar commonplaces for interpretation.

I have learned that success with literary anthropological methods, to a large extent, depends on the reader's ability to annotate the text that is being read. In the research I have reported in this chapter, for example, it was critical that I have access to the same copy of *Fugitive Pieces* for my multiple readings in order to notice how my perceptions and interpretations were evolving. Like the artifacts I have collected representing my mother's and my own lived experiences, these textual markings create moorings around which past experiences, and the interpretations of those experiences are organized and, importantly, where new interpretations might emerge.

One of the most challenging aspects of the development of literary anthropology as a response and research method has been to learn how to represent the complexity of the "commonplaces" that are developed during the reading and interpretation processes. How is it possible to create interpreted responses which present insights developed from literary anthropological methods that include some reference to the complex literary and nonliterary associations which enabled these insights, without overwhelming and/or confusing the reader with too many details? Further, how is it possible to create a text that presents insights while still retaining sufficient indeterminacy that challenges the reader to feel able to enlarge the interpretations?

Although the products of literary anthropological response methods always include references to and interpretations of literary characters and their situations, these are only presented to demonstrate how they have contributed to the development of ideas that are of interest to the reader. In the interpretive text presented earlier, for example, I discuss my identifications with and interpretations of characters and situations in *Fugitive Pieces* in order to point to insights that have been conditioned and influenced only in part by those identifications. Because my intention in this text is to foreground and interpret the relations between history and memory, and between language and geography, I must also present my identifications with other texts I have read, including theoretical and philosophical texts, and examples from my out-of-text experiences.

So that the insights created from these juxtapositional reading, response, and interpretive practices remain somewhat consistent with their influences, it is important that these engagements also be structured with sufficient indeterminacies so that the reader can become more explicitly involved in an interpretive collaboration with the author. Although I want to present some of the insights generated from my literary engagements, I also want to create an open text—one that offers sufficient information to condition and guide perception, without foreclosing possibilities for new understanding to be developed.

If these literary commonplaces are to become useful and interesting for others, however, they must be symbolized as artifacts that can live both alongside and after the life of the researcher. Just as Anne Michaels creates literary fiction to represent some of her critical conclusions and interpretations, I create texts that aim to function similarly. Over the years, my students, research collaborators and I have experimented with different ways to present our work and the insights emerging from this work. Although different writers develop unique styles, all of us have been able to create such artifacts using the basic method of anthropological inquiry that I have outlined in this chapter. The reading, marking, re-reading, re-marking, of literary texts, juxtaposed with engagements with non-literary texts, and other collected research data (autobiographical, biographical, ethnographic), creates the skeletal framework for interpretive work.

Alongside and following these reading and response activities we engage in what I call "interpretive linking." For the interpretive text presented in this chapter, for example, I began my work by trying to identify themes from *Fugitive Pieces* that were particularly compelling to me. In the early stages of my work, the phrase "Every moment is two moments" (referring to the confluence of history and memory) continued to present itself as interesting to me. During the time that I worked with this novel, I continued to study historical accounts of World War II, pragmatist philosophy, philosophical hermeneutics, and reader-response theory. In order to create small manageable pockets of interpretation, I took one quote from Anne Michaels' (1996) *Fugitive Pieces*, one statement from a memoir (for example, Peter Gay's (1998) *My German Question*) and one statement from a philosophical or theoretical text (for example, Rorty's (1999) *Philosophy and Social Hope*), typed these into a new computer file, and assigned myself a writing practice that attempted to link the three ideas together into some sort of interpretation. While not all of these assigned writing/interpretation practices yielded what I considered to be productive insights, many of them did. As these interpretive "puddles" were created, I printed them and filed them in a binder. Over a period of weeks, I continued the process of reading, re-reading, annotating, and re-annotating text and juxtaposing these with one another and with other experiences. As well, I assigned myself the task of creating short interpretive texts, which helped me to notice insights that were interesting and useful to me.

While I tend to repeat these processes, my final written products are always conditioned by other factors. For example, the text presented in this chapter was created while I was in the middle of making another move across the country, changing academic institutions, trying to interpret my relationship to events of World War II, and continuing the process of learning to understand the way my parents' experience continues in mine. By referring to my booknotes and, most importantly, developing my interpretive writing around ideas prompted by my identifications with characters from *Fugitive Pieces* and other texts, I eventually came to learn that in order to better understand some of my preoccupations, I needed to develop a larger analysis of the relationships among language, memory, history, and geography. These themes did not prompt my reading or early response and interpretive practices. Rather, they *emerged from* my ongoing re-reading of *Fugitive Pieces* and my continued practices of juxtaposing responses from this literary text to responses to other texts and other non-text experiences. The interpretive writing that I created presented some of the insights developed from my literary engagements and, as well, some description and discussion of influences that conditioned these engagements.

Over the years, I have come to understand that my teaching methods have both informed and been informed by literary anthropology reader-response methods. Although I did not know it during my years of teaching junior high school, when I asked my students to interpret their responses to literary fiction in relation to their own personal and collective experiences I was involving them in a kind of literary anthropology. In my more recent teaching of undergraduate and graduate students in education, I understand my insistence that we read novels alongside works of theory, philosophy, and history—followed by writing practices that ask them to create interpretations that link ideas from two or three of these—is another way of engaging in these research and interpretation practices.

I mention these pedagogical practices in order to highlight my belief that, while I present literary anthropology in this chapter as a research practice, I also use it and experience it as a pedagogical practice. This is not surprising since, for me, the research practices described are an important form of personal and cultural learning. In the interpretive writing presented earlier, the learning emerged from a deep engagement with cross-disciplinary and intergenerational representations and interpretations of other people's and my own experiences. In juxtaposing my literary engagements with material from other sources, I created conditions for a personal interpretation of much larger historical and cultural events. In beginning with the particularities of autobiographical and biographical experience, and developing historical and theoretical narratives around these, I have attempted to perform an important form of cultural learning that is, in part, presented in the "report" of my research.

It has been interesting for me to interpret a critical relationship with the events emerging from my parents' immigration to Canada following the Second World War. This is not so much because of what I have learned about them or myself but, rather, because of what I have learned about how large and small events of history continue to weave themselves into the contemporary world. Although these insights are personal, they also contribute to collective knowledge. As I come to more clearly understand my relationship to the historical, the geographical, and the social and cultural, I develop new interpretive tools that help me in my daily situations.

CHAPTER FIVE

Learning How to Fall in Love

CHAPTER SIX

While waiting in line to buy my groceries, I usually scan the front covers of popular magazines. Three topics dominate: sex, love, and dieting. Of course, these topics are thematically related. As the popular narrative goes, one needs to be thin to be attractive, attractive to be considered sexy, and sexy to fall in love. If these cultural myths are to be believed, falling in love is something that occurs naturally, not something that is learned.

As is the case with most children, in my early years I internalized these myths. For me, much of this learning emerged from relations I developed with school basal readers. Weren't all families supposed to be like Dick and Jane's? As a child who attended Catholic churches and schools, I was also convinced that the quintessential family was Mary, Joseph and Jesus. That Jesus, apparently, was "immaculately conceived" was one of the contradictions I ignored in order to create a seamless understanding of what the world was like. I also watched a lot of television, learning that falling in love could be something like what I noticed on shows like "The Brady Bunch" or "Leave it to Beaver." If falling in love (and staying in love) was accurately portrayed in the books I read and the television shows I watched, then no one I knew was in love.

But of course this was not so. Whenever I visited my aunt and uncle who lived "down east" (our way, in western Canada, of referring to anything east of the province of Manitoba), I knew I was in the presence of two persons who were in love. It was not their habit of hand-holding that convinced me of this as much as it was the mutual interest they seemed to be able maintain in particular projects: the small business they owned, the music they played and sang, the meals they prepared. In my more recent visits to them I realize that in retirement they have found new projects to collect and support their affection for one another: caring for their grandchildren, gardening, maintaining their real estate investments. For my Aunt Rita and Uncle Heinz, love is not an object thrown between them that must be continually tended; rather, love exists as an inextricable quality of their shared world.

It seems to me that most of us don't really know when we're in love, but we do seem to know when we're not. We are particularly aware of times when we *were* in love. I did not know, for example, that I loved my first partner of 12 years until after we had parted. Only then did I notice how much I missed our daily contact. Realizing this has helped me to maintain my current relationship. Rather than trying to locate my emotional attachment to my partner in a large feeling that might be called "being in love," I find it by noticing the many ways in which my fondness circulates in the small details of our shared lives. Love is organized by the small stories of lived experience, not by grand narratives of romantic love.

This is true, as well, for familial love. Although I knew I loved my mother, I did not know *how* I loved her until the last weeks before her death. As I spent time with her during her final days, what Elizabeth Hay (2000) in her novel *A Student of Weather* calls an "apartment of emotion" was erected in my consciousness. Because I had learned, by then, that love lives in details, I spent my last days with my mother paying attention to them. I was no longer bored or annoyed when she retold small stories from her childhood. I became interested in her new "hospital family" and learned to be attentive to the relationships that were developing. It was this understanding which, at several points during her final weeks, helped me to advocate on her behalf when doctors tried to move her from one ward of the hospital to the other. While they were primarily interested in her physical care, I knew that what mattered were her already-established relationships with people. "She does not need to make any more new friends," I argued. In the end, my mother and I did not express our love by continually affirming to one another that we loved one another (although there was some of that). We grew in love by attending to projects of immediate importance and significance.

These lessons of love have taught me to pay attention to the details of my experience with other people, particularly those with whom I am most intimate. It seems, then, that one does not only need to learn to fall in love, one needs to learn to *recognize* when one is in love. This is not as easy as it might seem. As I have experienced it through my relations with other persons and with fictional and biographical characters, being in the middle of love usually means that the feeling of love becomes transparent, unnoticed. It is only when love is withheld or missing that one understands its boundaries.

It seems that enduring love does not happen suddenly, nor does it occur in ways suggested by overly familiar narratives about falling in love. The belief that falling in love involves nothing other than meeting the "right person at the right time" positions events of love alongside lotteries and other games of chance— not an optimistic view for anyone aiming for loving attachments. This narrative suggests that falling in love is a prerequisite for ultimate bonding with a life partner. Most crucially, falling in love—if and when it happens—creates a bedrock for happiness. It is not surprising, then, that the idea of falling in love collects so much cultural worry and anxiety. Because falling in love is tied to happiness, the prospect of not finding the "right one" is frightening. How can one be complete or fully achieved without the experience of romantic love? Although it is acknowledged that most human activities must be learned, falling in love is understood as something innate, almost instinctual. As a result, falling in love has been reduced to some coincidental meeting of the biological and the experiential.

If falling in love is a learning experience, then understanding what it means to fall in love requires that some theory of learning be applied to its processes. Following Culler (1997), I define theory as something invented by humans that calls into question what most people believe to be "commonsense" understanding. Theory is intimately tied to different philosophic traditions that, while usually explicitly developed and circulated in academic settings, eventually work their ways into mainstream popular culture. All human thinking and action emerges alongside the theoretical narratives that are used to describe them. Because theory is entwined with everyday activity and language it is usually invisible and remains in the background of human experience. Although there are many contesting theories that are influential to human thought and action, there continues to be one tradition that, stubbornly, dominates.

Despite the fact that it has been contested for some years now in the academy, philosophic traditions that emerge from the work of Plato continue to organize popular beliefs about the relationships among humans, their contexts of experience, and the making and using of knowledge. Central to these Western philosophic traditions is a belief in "Reason." The idea of Reason has become foundational to the belief that "Truth" exists outside human experience. Human beings, it seems, are challenged to develop Reason in order to hone their capacities to seek and/or discern the world as it "really is." This valorizing of Reason has supported the creation of conditions that have allowed humans to believe themselves to be miraculously detached from the ecological and spiritual worlds. Among other problems, this theoretical belief has supported the continued mass destruction and abuse of the planet and biosphere, and an enduring belief in the superiority of the human species. While pre-modern human beings believed themselves to be in the midst of an ecologic and cosmic system that, in large part, was out of their control, we moderns erroneously believe that we can eventually, as 17th century philosopher and scientist Francis Bacon so charmingly suggested, "torture nature's secrets from her" for our own purposes. Just as we believe that nature's truths can be excised by Reason so, too, do we believe that love can be found.

In order to support this grand myth of Reason and its ability to eventually learn all of nature's secrets, we moderns have created a theory for what constitutes learning and a theory for what constitutes the self. It goes something like this: Learning means developing one's capacities to become aware of what truths exist outside our experience so that these might become useful in our development. From this theoretical perspective, learning is preoccupied with developing innate human qualities in order to accumulate information. The more information the human subject can accumulate, the closer she or he will be to understanding the "truths" of the universe. Learning, then, is not a project of accommodating to one's contexts; it is a project of learning to control them. It is not surprising, then, that most of us believe that love is out there somewhere, and that in order to achieve it we need to find it using our developed perceptual and interpretive skills. In order to change the way falling in love is understood, these no-longer-very-useful theories about how people learn things must be abandoned in favor of a more complex understanding of learning.

Although many readers may not interpret it as a "love story" Martha Brooks' (1997) novel *Bone Dance* shows how love emerges from the tangled relations of memory, personal and cultural history. Set in the Canadian prairie province of Manitoba, *Bone Dance* explores how teenagers Alexandra Sinclair and Lonny LaFreniere learn about love. Developed around each of their journeys to learn about unknown parents and family and personal secrets, this novel reminds readers that one's experience, in large part, is structured by histories that are not of one's own making. Primary to the argument I present in this chapter is the suggestion that this loving attachment does not develop in ways represented by commonsense discourses of romantic love.

Bone Dance reminds readers that human consciousness is multilayered and recursive. It does not march forever forward but, rather, achieves its moments of awareness from overlapping loops of memory, present perception, and future imaginings. Cultural artifacts such as books, photographs, art, music, and letters are examples of the objects that serve to collect memory and history and, ultimately, that function to organize human identity. This novel shows that a sense of self is not so much enveloped by one's skin but, rather, exists more ambiguously in the relations among memory, history, language, and objects of the human made and more-than-human world. A human being identifies her or himself and is identified by others through involvement in intricate webs of relations. When we say "I know that person" or "I know myself" what we are really saying is "I know something about how that person is involved in the world" or "I have a coherent understanding of how I am involved in the world."

Of course, knowing about worldly relations is often not as easy as it might seem. In *Bone Dance*, readers learn that Alexandra is a 17-year-old Métis woman who has never met her White father, Earl McKay. But she has a relationship with him nonetheless, one that has been developed through stories her mother tells, and from occasional letters she receives from him. Although the persona of her father is largely invented through the interpretive tasks of piecing together these narratives and letters, for Alexandra the relationship she has with Earl is not less influential than those she has with other persons.

Alexandra's imagined relationship to her father contributes, in important ways, to the identity that she continually forges for herself. Like all human beings who engage in daily acts of inventing information to overcome gaps in their knowledge, Alexandra pieces together various narratives and other experiences that circulate around her, and from these distills an ongoing sense of self identity. Her eventual partner in love, Lonny LaFreniere, must also do some inventing to create his own identity. Not only has he never known his biological father, but also because his mother dies shortly after her marriage to his stepfather, he must rely on family and community stories to maintain connections to his biological and cultural heritage.

Through these characters, *Bone Dance* shows readers that identity not only emerges from what is presently known but, to a great extent, is affected by what is present, but not represented. For both Lonny and Alexandra, family and personal secrets participate in the ways in which they organize and express personal and cultural knowledge.

These secrets have an effect. As I discussed in Chapter Five, secrets become strongly influential to the ways in which one organizes one's life. For Alexandra and Lonny, the existence of secret knowledge creates a kind of emotional anesthesia, an inability to make direct and deep contact with others. In order to restore feeling, they must learn about and represent the secrets that have been structuring their experiences. However, contrary to what is commonly believed, the unveiling of secrets is not simply a matter of telling the truth. A precursor to learning about (and from) secret knowledge is the creating of conditions for the development of insight.

For Alexandra, these conditions present themselves when she makes a journey to visit the property her father left to her. It is here she learns from a letter he wrote, and which she received after his death, that he was addicted to alcohol for most of his life. With this family secret revealed, Alexandra begins to understand his absence from her life. She develops further insight by spending time alone in the cabin he built and lived in during his last years. For Alexandra this is like living in an archive. However, in order to interpret this archive, she must learn some new skills. The most important and difficult one, it seems, is to begin to notice the small details of her father's life. This is not possible by relying on visual perception. It is not merely examining her father's life objects that help her to understand him. Instead, Alexandra finds that she must incorporate these objects into her daily living practices. Wearing her father's leather jacket that she finds hanging on a hook behind a door, using his kitchen utensils, sitting in his chair while looking at the view that was previously his, and walking the trails created by his footsteps helps her to understand him and his contexts. As Alexandra's knowledge about her father is elaborated, she begins to develop new personal insights. Most importantly, she comes to learn that life seems small only if it is not understood as connected to dying. As Alexandra continues to interpret her place in history, she feels herself coming home.

Lonny's project of personal reconciliation is more difficult, since it requires the telling of a secret from his boyhood, one involving curiosity and the excavation of bones from the ancient burial ground located on what is now Alexandra's land. Because this act closely precedes the sudden death of his mother, Lonny comes to believe that his ancestors are punishing him for desecrating their graves. For Lonny, this secret becomes a collecting place for growing uncertainty about his position in his family and community. Adrift with secret knowledge, he moves through the world without developing deep emotional bonds with others. Although he has many sexual contacts with women, and develops a number of casual friendships with men, these skirt the surface of his consciousness, never becoming rooted in deep and committed ways.

Although there are many explanations that can be offered for Lonny's ongoing experiences of alienation, I believe that many of his difficulties emerge from the curious ways secrecy has organized his experiences. As covert knowledge, Lonny's secret remains unchanged and, therefore, so must the small stories he creates around that secret. Unlike other experiential narratives that continually shift and accommodate to current and imagined circumstances, the structures supporting secrecy remain fixed. These fixed structures of covert knowledge become foundational to Lonny's experience, continually inhibiting his ability to invent a more generous and flexible sense of self-identity. I believe it is this that prevents him from experiencing the deep satisfaction of love. Before Lonny can fall in love, he must learn that experiences of loving others depend upon learning to enlarge the boundaries of one's self to accommodate other narratives. Before love can occur, Lonny's tangle of secrecy must be dissolved.

Bone Dance helps readers to understand that because love is always influenced by history and by present circumstances, it is not really something that is carried *inside* lovers. Love is something that exists in the relationships people develop with one another. This is not, as commonly believed, a relationship that is founded upon each of the lover's already-known and represented identities but, rather, is one that emerges from some project of involvement that exceeds each of their individual selves. Whatever the project—whether it is running the family farm, writing books together, raising children, or some combination of shared activities—it is the *project* that becomes the collecting place for affection between two persons. Love needs lovers to be interested in something other than themselves or each other—something that, paradoxically, requires that conditions be created for lovers to become attentive to and caring to one another.

Of course, loving relations are also influenced by biology. While sexual attraction is strongly influenced by culture, like all species, humans are drawn to one another for reasons that exceed cultural interpretations. Whether these are opposite- or same-sex attractions, most human beings know the phenomenon of being strongly drawn to another human. Typically followed by a period of what is known as "infatuation"—a state where biological and experiential components of attraction collect into a pleasurable obsession—for many couples sexual attraction becomes one of the cornerstones of loving relationships. It is important to remember, however, that infatuation is not love, at least not the kind of love that is experienced by Lonny and Alexandra.

For these characters, the difference between infatuation and love might be described as the difference between the experience of feeling strong attraction to another human being and one of developing an interpreted understanding of one's relationship with someone. Infatuation, as Lonny had experienced it with women before Alexandra, required the Other be continually present (either physically or psychologically) in order for the relationship to continue. What Lonny failed to understand was that love does not require sexual contact, but it does depend upon some ongoing project.

Bone Dance shows that human beings can experience love by learning how to create conditions for love to develop. Most important, *Bone Dance* helps its readers to understand that falling in love is always a historical and interpretive cultural act. Love collects more than just the lovers; love collects the complexity of their many worldly attachments, including those that live in memory. The strong desire human beings have to fall in love, then, is not really a selfish desire. Falling in love can be a deeply moral and ethical act. In caring for and loving each other, human beings must dissolve the boundaries of their own carefully crafted identities. This is not merely an act of attention to another person. As the characters in *Bone Dance* learn, it is a deeply spiritual and ecological act.

As is common in most university settings, my colleagues and I are required to have students write evaluations of our courses and our teaching abilities. Most of us have mixed feelings about these, since, as one of my colleagues has noticed, course evaluations are often either "love letters" or "hate mail." While this may be overstating the case, it has certainly been my experience that when asked, students are usually unable to extricate the subject matter from their experienced relationship with their teacher. While there are certainly those evaluations that exist somewhere in between the "love letter" and "hate mail" categories, I have noticed that students' remarks about courses I have taught are often polarized in this way.

These experiences of love and hate are not confined to university settings. Because I teach in a Faculty of Education, I have many opportunities to notice how events of learning are organized by interpersonal attachments and emotions. Although I notice this in my work with beginning teachers and experienced teachers in schools, I become most keenly aware of it each year when I ask my teacher candidates to critically reflect on their past experience with teachers by writing descriptive narratives of events of learning that have mattered to them. While I never explicitly ask them to write about teachers, they nearly always do.

In examining some of the narratives my students have written over the years, it has become clear that common to most of them is an attention to what the teacher has asked students to learn. Favorite teachers seem to help students become interested in particular subjects: "I love math because of Mrs. Williams." "I became an artist because of what Mr. Ford taught me." "I learned to love music from Mrs. Melling." Although the students claim to love their teacher, most of their narratives do not describe teachers but, rather, describe what the teachers made significant.

When students read these narratives of favorite teachers in class, I ask them what they remember about the teachers. They usually respond by telling me more about what teachers asked them to do in class. I always must press them to think past these pedagogical practices. "What did you know about *them*?" In most instances, students know almost nothing about these teachers. This is not surprising, given the fact that the world of school, for both students and teachers, is a world unto itself, one that is only loosely connected to "not school." They do not know much about their favorite teachers, and yet they love them. Or so they say. It seems to me that they love what they and the teacher have become interested in. They loved what happened in the science lab. They loved the challenge of solving mathematical problems. They loved what they learned about history or geography. They loved being interested in something with someone else.

But, of course, there is more to it than this. Also embedded in the narratives of good teachers that students write are references to the curiosity of the teacher. This is usually first represented as an interest in the student, the writer of the narrative: "My teacher was interested in me. He took time to find out about me." When asked to elaborate, however, most of my students cannot recall specific instances where the teacher has probed for personal details. Instead, what they describe is the teacher's interest in what is studied and how this was made personally relevant to the student.

I have come to believe that the narratives beginning teachers write about favorite teachers are expressions of a complex loving attachment. They are narratives that represent a strong feeling of emotional and psychic bond that students have felt (and continue to feel) for some of their teachers. We could call this feeling love. The kind of love my students are writing about is not unlike the love depicted in *Bone Dance*. It is a love that emerges from the hard work of making something with other people.

Although it is shocking to my students, I tell them great teachers love what they are teaching more than they love their students. This does not mean that they do not care for their students, nor does it mean that they do not develop strong feelings of attachment to them. Instead, it means that good teachers understand that if people are to become committed to one another, they need a shared project. The teacher's most important work is to create conditions whereby students are able to enter into a world of inquiry that is new and interesting. At the same time, the good teacher understands that if this world of inquiry is to remain interesting to the teacher, its boundaries must be continually expanded to include what is not familiar to the teacher. Good teaching, then, depends upon the teacher's ability to create conditions whereby she and her students can enter into a shared world of inquiry that, while primarily organized by her, is also able to accommodate what students know and, importantly, what is generated through their shared interest. If teachers love what they are teaching, and invite students into an inquiry of that subject matter, both the teacher and the students will experience love.

In *Fugitive Pieces* (1996) the character Jakob Beer suggests, "if you learn to love one landscape, you can learn to love others" (p. 82). Learning to love a landscape, like learning to love anything, means learning its details and noticing the way in which one's involvement with those details is interesting and influential. Unfortunately, familiarity obscures detail and that is why so many people do not love the landscapes to which they have become habituated. In order to learn to love a landscape, one must pay attention to it.

This has become more apparent to me in recent years. Although I grew up in the middle of the Canadian prairies, I did not love them until I learned to walk through unfarmed grasslands with attention. I needed to try to notice what was in front of me, rather than walking for fitness or walking to appreciate the wide horizon of a prairie sky. While both of these are worthwhile, they do not challenge what is immediately present to conscious perception. In order to learn to love a prairie landscape, I needed to walk in the prairies with my friend Pat and her Labrador retriever, Sophie. Like all dogs, Sophie is only interested in details and, through her interest, I came to notice features of the prairie that had previously been invisible to me. And, because Pat has decided to become knowledgeable about native plants, through her interest I am learning a vocabulary to accompany my newfound loving attachment to a prairie landscape. As we meander up and down the prairie trails, stopping to pay attention to what Sophie is noticing, I am learning to love the prairies and, at the same time, I am deepening my affection for my long-time friend. Learning how to fall in love with a landscape means paying attention to and learning about its details. Sharing this project with someone can deepen loving attachments to other people.

These skills of attention and discernment can be honed from textual engagement practices. In her essay "The Ethics of Close Reading" Jane Gallop (2000) describes and analyzes close reading practices she teaches her university students. While she makes a number of interesting points, the one most relevant for arguments I am presenting in this chapter is her insistence that it is important to teach students how to attend to the marks on the page made by the writer. In asking students to notice and interpret details of the text that are usually not noticed (footnotes, repeated phrases and images, etc.), Gallop is doing what all teachers must do: pointing to aspects of the world that students might not notice. In asking students to attend to details, Gallop is asking them to learn the topography of the text. She is not asking them to fall in love with the text, or to fall in love with her. As students learn to notice and interpret the particularity of a textual topography they create the possibility for an interesting interpretive site that was not previously available to them.

Of course, learning to notice the small details of a text means that it needs to be read carefully, and usually a few times. Importantly, it needs to be read over time. These re-reading activities create conditions in which aspects of one's out-of-text lived experiences become partly structured by repeated textual involvements. Immersing oneself in the details of a textual landscape can create conditions whereby other landscapes of one's life become more interesting. In curious ways, an attention to textual details can create a deep loving attachment to that text. Following Anne Michaels, I contend that one needs to learn to love *one* landscape in order to love others. If human identities are considered topographies whose details must be first perceived in order to be deeply known, then it seems that requisite to falling in love (and staying in love) is to learn to notice and interpret the details of one's relations with another person. Like all interpretive practices, then, learning to fall in love requires some experience and some learned skills.

Literary engagement creates conditions for some of these interpretation skills to be learned. Learning to identify with literary characters means learning to notice how they are not identical to the reader. And, because literary characters continue to be presented identically each time the text is read, they offer the reader an opportunity to notice how her or his own perceptions continue to change. However, the kind of deep learning and insight that can emerge from literary identifications usually requires the reader to enter into a committed, mindful and sustained literary engagement. Ideally, this means that readers do not skim texts but, rather, read them slowly and carefully, trying to notice how details are used to create literary effects. It also means that readers need to consider re-reading texts since, of course, the familiar features of the text cannot usually be seen on a first reading. In order for the topography of the text to be more deeply interpreted, it needs to be negotiated more than once.

These close reading practices have the potential to teach readers how to become attentive to details that shape perception. Although readers probably experience this as an attachment to literary characters, I suggest that what is experienced is actually fondness for what the relationship sponsors—an interpretive site where personal insight is generated.

In this chapter, I have argued that learning to fall in love means becoming involved with someone in projects that require ongoing attention to details. Staying in love means maintaining some interpretive interest. Because familiarity obscures one's perception of details, staying in love also means deliberately interrupting what has become habitually familiar with new interpretive challenges. People often become bored or restless or fall out of love because the details that make them interesting to one another have grown invisible. Falling in love with literary characters, with landscapes, with subject matter, with other people, requires an ongoing commitment to attending to the details of how those relations are conditioned and structured. As I have argued, once we no longer perceive the details of our relations, it is difficult to maintain strong emotion. In order for strong emotion to be restored, it is important for familiarity to become interrupted. Sometimes this means that someone needs to point to something that we haven't noticed before: "Look at that! Isn't that interesting!"

Sometimes our attention must be directed to something that has become invisible because it is overly familiar. This, of course, has always been the work of art. Historically speaking, the art object functions to both interrupt and enlarge perception. A poem can only become a poem, for example, if it asks readers to pay attention to the vocabulary and the form in which it presents itself. "I'm a poem. And although I am made of words you know, I want you to pay attention to those words in new ways." Or, "I'm a painting. Even though this is a painting of something you know as a tree, I want you to notice details of 'tree-ness' that you had not noticed before."

As a work of art, literature asks readers to pay attention to the details that organize the experience of literary engagement. In so doing, the literary text creates possibilities for readers to become involved with the author and characters she or he has created in the ongoing project of learning something new. In order for the literary text to do its work well, the reader needs to pay attention to the details of the text, to read carefully, to think about what is read, to wonder about what this means and, probably, to re-read and think about how re-reading affects one's involvement with characters and their situations.

Many of us have forgotten that in order to love anything we must learn *how* to fall in love. In a world that has decided that having access to a lot of information is more valuable than developing committed and ongoing relationships to small amounts of subject matter, it is more difficult to fall in love with anything or anyone. Why re-read books when I have access to new books I haven't read? Why study with one teacher when I can access unlimited information from the Internet using powerful search engines? Why learn to love one person when I can make many on-line contacts with new and exciting people?

One way to learn to fall in love with another person might be to learn to fall in love with other things. This might mean, as Jeanette Winterson (1995) has suggested in her book of essays *Art Objects*, learning to spend time with one painting rather than rushing through a museum looking at all the paintings. It might mean, as Sharon Butala (1994) suggests in *The Perfection of the Morning* learning how to love a landscape by attending to and learning about its details. It might mean, as Kathleen Norris (1993) argues in *Dakota* learning to understand that human perception and thinking is not only organized by human-made objects but, as well, is influenced by the non-human-made world. It might mean, as Buddhist monk Thich Nhat Hahn (1991) suggests in *Peace is Every Step* meditating on one's own breathing, trying to calm the constant noise of the mind.

I have learned my lessons of love by developing relationships with literary texts. In reading and re-reading and thinking about my attachments to characters and their situations, I have created focal practices that help me to better understand my own situation. I have not learned to fall in love with other people by studying them or myself directly. I am able to love them because my own unhurried and close reading practices have taught me how to notice usually unnoticed details that circumscribe my experience. In so doing, I have learned that love is not out there to be found nor is love some object that can be made. Instead, love emerges from work I share with other people.

CHAPTER SIX

Interpreting Identities:
Enlarging the Space of the Possible

CHAPTER SEVEN

Like Chapters Three and Five, this chapter is primarily interested in examining the complexity of human identity, and in noticing how this complexity is both created and interpreted by particular practices. As with the first two performative texts, my reading of a novel created the commonplace within which my interpretations were developed. When I read and re-read Mark Salzman's (2000) novel *Lying Awake*, I was provoked to examine artifacts collected during a Catholic Retreat I attended as a high school student and to wonder about how certain rituals can create conditions whereby familiar perceptions can become interrupted. My intention in this chapter is to elaborate the ways in which rituals can interrupt familiarity and offer the potential for human beings to enlarge the space of what seems possible.

As I worked on this writing, I felt compelled to offer concluding statements. I thought that perhaps I ought to reiterate points I had alluded to in the chapter, particularly those that hinted at the importance of ritual, the significance of "the mysteries," or the value of meditation. In the end, however, I decided that if this text were to "enlarge the space of the possible" I had to resist the urge to complete the interpretive circle. Like the novelist who creates characters to enact ideas that eventually are controlled as much by the reader as they are by the author, I offer this chapter as a partial representation of thinking that requires the reader's engagement before any conclusions can be drawn.

March, 1976, Lethbridge, Alberta. I am walking down a candle-lit hallway of my high school, which, for this weekend, has been transformed into a location for a Catholic religious retreat. There are about thirty of us in the procession, mostly grade twelve students, several nuns who are also teachers in the school, and one priest. We are singing, "Make Me a Channel of Your Peace" and moving through the "Stations of the Cross," a series of images depicting Jesus' journey to crucifixion and resurrection.

At each station we stop and stand silently as Father Watrin reads the scripture that accompanies the image. At some point during this ritual, I begin to feel disoriented, light-headed. I am not sure what this means. Will I faint? The feeling persists until it collects into a rush of emotion that runs through my entire body. I wonder if this is Jesus speaking to me. Or am I just exhausted? Perhaps 2 days confined indoors, without television, radio, clocks, or any contact at all with the world outside the retreat, coupled with sleep deprivation, and continuous participation in unfamiliar rituals and routines have made me giddy. Maybe I'm hallucinating. Whether by divine intervention or simply from the effects of fatigue, I feel content and happy.

The next morning I am energized. I continue to feel physical traces of my experience of the previous night. Although I have not discussed it with anyone, I can see that my peers are also excited, eager to continue with the last day at the retreat. I begin to believe something important has happened.

CHAPTER SEVEN

January, 2001, Edmonton, Alberta. I am reading Mark Salzman's (2000) novel *Lying Awake*, the story of a cloistered Carmelite nun, Sister John of the Cross. After many years of religious confinement, Sister John finally experiences what is perceived by her as God and is able to create large amounts of writing that represents and interprets these spiritual events. At the height of her spiritual and literary powers, Sister John begins to experience debilitating migraines, which are eventually associated with a rare form of epilepsy caused by a small tumor in her cerebral cortex. In addition to pain, she learns that other common symptoms include hypergraphia (voluminous writing), an intensification and narrowing of emotional response, and an obsessive interest in religion and philosophy. She learns that Dostoevsky, an epileptic, had these symptoms and that Van Gogh, Tennyson, and Proust are believed to have suffered the same condition. Unlike these historical figures, who learned to live with their symptoms, Sister John is told that a relatively uncomplicated surgical procedure will eliminate the petit mal seizures that create her symptoms. Of course, eliminating the physical pain associated with this disorder would also mean abandoning the conditions that have structured experiences Sister John considers spiritual and, at the same time, would abruptly halt her ability to write about them.

As I read about Sister John, I feel the hair rise on my arms. I have migraines. Although I do not write about a relationship with God when I emerge from my hazy white storm, I am able to create new focus with current writing projects. Usually the exit of a migraine creates a window of insight that unravels some knot I am trying to untangle in my thinking. I wonder if I have a brain tumor. I decide this is something I must think about investigating. However, like Sister John, if there is a growth on my cerebral cortex that helps to create conditions for my creative work, I am loath to have it removed. How would I organize my experience if I could not stitch it together with reading and writing?

January, 2001, Edmonton, Alberta. I am writing about my experience of reading *Lying Awake*, and making connections between this literary experience, Sister John's epilepsy and her relationship with Jesus, and my recent re-reading of letters I received from friends and relatives at a Catholic retreat I attended during my last year of high school. As I type I feel hypnotized by the words appearing on the screen. I am exhilarated. I realize that the physical responses I am experiencing during this moment of interpretive writing are almost identical to those I have when in the middle of generating some sort of insight from reading books that I like. Often these books are novels, but just as often they are memoirs, philosophical arguments, or works of theory.

March, 1976, Lethbridge, Alberta. The retreat is over and my stepfather is driving me home. The sun is too bright, the street too wide. I yearn for the closeness of the retreat. When we arrive home, I claim fatigue and immediately excuse myself to my room, although I am not tired. I sit on my bed and re-read my letters. I notice that my room is small and cluttered. For the first time, it seems insufficient. I hear my mother and stepfather arguing upstairs about some matter I consider minor. I feel caught in the web of their relationship. At the same time, I feel less attached to them and our shared circumstances. This is satisfying to me. I know that the world of this family and this house can be transgressed without leaving it. The space of what seems possible has been enlarged and I am grateful for that. I re-read the scripture that I transcribed on a card before leaving the retreat. I decide that I can believe what I imagine, not just what I see. Although I did not know it then, I realize now that this insight has likely saved my life.

January, 2001, Edmonton, Alberta. My involvement with the character Sister John helps me to understand that the positive effects of my high school religious retreat were not so much organized by what we humans have come to call God but, rather, by the conditions created for those of us who participated in such removals from the familiar world to invent a needed relationship to the "mysteries." As I now reflect upon that event, I am amazed at the audacity of my teachers who organized and created the structures for these retreats. During a time in our young lives when we sought certainty (Who will I marry? Who will love me? What career will I have? How can I respond to those who hurt me?), we were thrown into the arms of ambiguity. While one might argue that religious retreats create another kind of certainty ("If you love God and surrender yourself to His will you will find peace and happiness."), my small experience of immersion at this retreat suggests to me that the opposite is true: In asking human subjects to believe in something that is unseen, unknown, unrepresentable, the world of spirituality asks modern citizens to give up the idea of certainty.

The challenge to submit to a more-than-human spirituality is not confined to Christians. Whether one organizes spiritual life around the teachings of Jesus or Buddha or Mohammed, the key to the sort of productive spirituality that I am thinking of is not so much reverence to a person, or a spiritual being, or a set of dogmas but, rather, is a daily lived belief that there are some things that humans cannot know or, at least, that humans will never find language to describe or fully interpret.

March, 1976, Lethbridge, Alberta. It is Saturday night, 24 hours since we arrived at the retreat. I am pleasantly tired. It has been a full day of prayer, singing, and meditation. There have been periods of the day when I have been asked to perform different tasks on my own: reading scripture, writing responses, meditating upon a particular idea, sitting quietly. Juxtaposed with this isolation are communal meals, group mass and prayer services, and attendance at testimonials given by some of my peers who made retreats earlier in the year.

Now, during the time that I would usually be at home watching TV, working at my job as a baker's helper in a local supermarket, or partying with my friends, I am handed a packet of letters addressed to me, written by different people I know. This surprises me. We are told to find a private place to read these letters and to reflect on what their contents mean to us.

January, 2001, Edmonton, Alberta. In preparing to write about what it was like to receive and read these letters at the retreat, I spend an hour re-reading them. I have eighteen letters, equally divided between those written by peers and those written by teachers and other adults in my life. I have a letter from the mother of a young woman I was dating at the time. She includes a hand-written copy of a religious poem and she thanks me for being so considerate to her daughter. I have a letter from my stepfather, most of which is a prose excerpt copied from something that he already owned with a sentence of his own at the end, encouraging me to work hard and do well. I remember feeling disappointed and relieved that my mother did not write a letter. One letter is from a friend who chastises me for being too eager to accommodate to others' wishes.

I have a few letters from teachers. One is from the school librarian, a woman I hardly know. She writes about her own interpretation of what spirituality means. I cannot recall what I thought of it in 1976. Today, I am struck by one of her sentences: "Two key attitudes in our search for the Lord in our life are silence and joy." I know that one gift writing has given me is the opportunity to sequester myself in silence for several hours a day while I write and read and think. The word "joy," however, is not one that I use to describe my experience. Instead, I wonder if I am happy, concluding that I probably am, but that I cannot find ways to use language to create a representative shape for happy. Joy, on the other hand, echoing words like "rejoice" or the French "jouissance" feels like pleasure, gratitude, celebration.

Another is from my former Grade One teacher, a woman I knew as Sister Mary Louise but who eventually left the convent. As I reread this letter it occurs to me that she is now in her mid sixties. I remember her face and her hands clearly, likely because this was all that was visible, the rest of her shrouded by the black habit she wore every day. To my 6-year-old eyes, Sister Mary Louise was perfection incarnate and I loved her. I know that the "most improved student award" I received at the end of Grade One represented my efforts to please her. Although promotion to Grade Two meant a new teacher, I continued to visit Sister Mary Louise every day after school, helping with small tasks.

Reading these letters helps me to understand why my Grade Twelve year was remarkable, and why I continue to feel such a strong attachment and commitment to that experience and to the persons I knew during that time. In choosing to create relationships around something that we could not "see" or could not explain in human terms—something that was organized by ethics of care, love and consideration—we learned how to continually interrupt the certainty of our daily lived situations and the usual imperative to focus only on individual development.

While I am not a participating Catholic, I have continued to organize my life around a deeply held conviction that it is crucial for humans to refuse to believe in the supremacy of the human subject. For me this has meant remembering that human beings simply cannot simultaneously participate in the world of their experience and, at the same time, be fully and mindfully aware of the fullness of that participation. Although I can provide informed descriptions and interpretations of my experience, which utilize insights learned from research and personal experience, I understand that these experiences, in large measure, are organized by what I do not notice. Although it is popularly believed that human beings must understand their contexts in order to function effectively, it is largely the case that most of our daily experience is maintained through acts of imagination and invention. As I drive down the freeways that crisscross the city in which I live, for example, I do not know what everyone else is doing or thinking, nor can I be aware of what's around the next corner. While rules of the road create some conditions to support my ability to drive safely, like all drivers I also depend on acts of faith and invention. As with any act of human conversation, where meaning is continually shifted through a dance of dialogic exchange (Gadamer, 1990), shared activity requires an ongoing evolution of a structural relationship (Maturana & Varela, 1987). That one should be able to proceed without knowing everything that influences one's experiences means that human existence is always, to a large extent, a surprise, not a plan.

May, 1997. Tofino, British Columbia. It is the evening of the third day of our teacher research group's retreat. Guided by structures created by our colleague Rebecca Luce-Kapler, we have produced writing that we are now reading aloud to the group. Terry, who recently underwent sex reassignment surgery, writes about her love of the natural spaces that still comprise the tiny amount of the North American Rain Forest located on the west coast of Vancouver Island where our cabins are located. Her writing is deeply moving, reminding us that we European-descended white people were not the first to lay claim to these lands. As others read poems, autobiographical narratives, and interpretations of ideas they have been thinking about over the last few days, I am struck with the intensity of our engagement with one another. While we had been meeting for a full day, once a month for 2 years prior to the retreat, it is not until tonight that we seem to have found new ways of understanding and expressing our experiences.

Sitting in this wood-paneled candle-lit room, the small roar of the open ocean outside our front door, we read writing that represents insights we have created. As I read my own writing, I feel a new fondness for my colleagues. And, as I look at the faces of the others, I realize that the same is occurring for them. No one is fidgeting, or merely waiting for his or her turn to read. Everyone is attentive, waiting for the next word to drop, wondering what it will mean when it does. When we are finished reading we sit quietly, nervously, not wanting to break the spell that has been created.

Understanding that this event needs personal interpretation before it is ruined by public pronouncements, Rebecca quietly asks us to take our writing journals and spend 1/2 hour writing. She does not tell us what to write, but by now we understand that the directive to write means to simply open our notebooks and start writing. The act of writing, we have learned, is an act of learning what needs to be learned.

The morning that we are to leave our cabins we are different people. Although our shared living experiences over the last few days created a communal bond that did not previously exist, our interpretation practices, and the rituals that conditioned these, have also made us strange to one another. We are quiet and tentative. I am anxious to enter into my old life with the new insights I have gained, but I am also reluctant to leave behind the conditions that made these insights possible. I understand, however, that if I were to stay here those conditions would quickly evaporate, since what made them possible was the fact that this place is not home, my colleagues are not my primary relational contacts, and the writing rituals we shared are not identical to those I would use at home.

In 1987, biologists and cognitive theorists Humberto Maturana and Francisco Varela published a small revolutionary book entitled *The Tree of Knowledge*, where they drew on recent discoveries in evolutionary biology, as well as insights from philosophy, to argue that the mind is not confined to the human brain. Several years later Varela co-authored a book with Evan Thompson and Eleanor Rosch (1991), which provided a more comprehensive account of how this view of mind was supported not only by recent scientific research but, as well, by the ancient Eastern wisdom traditions, particularly Buddhism.

In these works, the authors attempt to represent, academically, what human beings experience daily: the body and the mind are inextricable from one another. Further, they suggest that the individual human biological body is intimately entwined in other bodies: the social, the cultural, the epistemic. Their work suggests that in order to learn about human learning, researchers need to try to represent the complexity of the learner's involvement in these complicit systems. If I want to deeply understand what it means to be a reader, I cannot merely study the reader, the texts read, or the contexts of reading. Instead, I must invent ways to study the complex relations among these.

Different teachers develop different ways to do this. My friend and colleague Pat Chuchryk begins her research methods course by asking pairs of students to spend the first half hour of class interviewing one another. Then she asks them to sit back-to-back so that they cannot see one another and to list details about the other person: What color are the eyes? Are there earrings? What do they look like? Shirt or sweater? Jeans or skirt? Shoes or runners? Most students are quite inaccurate in their descriptions. What is perceived and remembered usually has little relation to what exists. This is not only a lesson about conducting research; it is a lesson about reading. As is now well known, readers are prone to projecting their interpretations and wishes on a text, even when the arguments presented discourage them. And it is a lesson of everyday life: Are things seen as they "really are" or are they perceived as the perceiver wants them to be?

Recent research in the science of perception (Norretranders, 1998; Pinker, 1997; Sacks, 1995) has clearly shown that in order for humans to be able to perceive, processes of discarding must be learned. This means that when we humans look at anything, we usually see what we expect to see. It is difficult to be surprised. Learning to notice something new usually means that it needs to be distinguished from the backdrop of what is usually ignored. That is why it is so interesting to go for a walk with someone who is either more familiar or less familiar with a landscape than we are (Butala, 1994; Norris, 1993). Those who have decided to learn about the details of a particular landscape can provide informed details: "This plant is called spear grass. This is a buffalo flower." Those who are new to a landscape usually notice larger things: "There are so many trees that I can't see the sky!" Or, as is common with those who are new to a prairie landscape: "Standing out here makes me dizzy! It all looks the same."

It seems that human beings do not merely "see" what's out there; human beings learn to see and, most importantly, in order to accomplish this, they learn how to "not see" most things in their immediate worlds of contact. It is this learned discarding process that allows each of us to negotiate our daily worlds without becoming exhausted. If the discarding process were not in effect, each day would be like visiting a strange land, which, as any traveler can attest, requires considerable energy.

The problem with creating conditions for a relatively effortless daily existence, however, is that familiarity often obscures the possibility to notice what is interesting. As Grumet (1991b) has explained, it is the major work of the teacher to "point" to aspects of the world that interrupt familiarity. And, as Gallop (2000) has suggested, this attention to detail must be learned.

In recent years I have been asking my pre-service undergraduate teacher education students to write about old shoes. At the beginning of the term I ask them to find a pair of old shoes of their own and bring them to class, concealed in bag. I insist that they do not show these shoes to other members of the class. I then redistribute the shoes, asking each class member to take home someone else's shoe and place it in a prominent place in their home—for example, on top of their computer monitor, on their bedroom dresser top, on the bathroom counter.

When they return the following week (with the shoe), I ask them to place the shoe on the table in front of them. Throughout these exercises, I continually remind them that they must not identify their own original shoe. I ask students what it was like to live with someone else's shoe. "It was strange!" "I found it disturbing and eventually had to put it in my closet". "It was like an invasion of someone else's and my privacy." "I felt like the shoe was watching me."

For the next several hours, I ask students to engage in short writing practices that try to create new contexts and situations for the shoe they have adopted: "Write about a place this shoe might have been." "Write about something this shoe might have done." I then ask each student to pair up with another to link these short narratives. "Tell each other the stories of where your shoe has been and what it has done and see what happens when you put these together." In every case, students invent interesting stories that reveal complex characters.

Although I use this activity to teach a lesson about identity (Identities are not innate, they are made.) and, as well, to teach something about creative writing (Characters emerge from settings and plots, they do not announce settings and plots.), I also use it to demonstrate to my students the importance of interrupting perceptions of the mundane objects and events that structure daily experiences. When students complain that the old shoe made them feel uncomfortable in their own home, and later when they produce rich narratives from imagined features that become attached to these shoes, they are learning to transgress the boundaries of what organizes their perceptual and interpretive worlds (Davis, Sumara, & Luce-Kapler, 2000).

This experience of boundary crossing becomes especially interesting when the owners of the old shoes bear witness to the new narratives that have been constructed around them by others in the class: "This was the shoe that I wore to my high school graduation. Now I'll never be able to look at it without remembering how it was involved in a passionate love affair on a cruise ship!"

Memory, it seems, is not only a representation of a particular event that happened in the past, it is also an interpretation of those images and narratives that have, over time, collected around that memory (Gadamer, 1990; Merleau-Ponty, 1962). As a cultural object, the shoes of my students become newly significant in ways that do not always please them: "That sandal was the one I wore during my year in South Asia. I'm not sure that I like the fact that for me it is now associated with a character who was, it seems, utterly loathsome! I'm going to try to forget I ever heard that!" Good luck. Whether the perceived attachments are explicit or rendered covert, seemingly not noticed or forgotten, they continue to influence the topography of thinking.

I mention my "old shoe" lessons in this chapter because, for me, this activity helps both my students and me to remember that while perception is structured by physiological abilities, it is continually organized and reorganized by experiences. As neurologists have shown, in order to see, human beings must *learn* to see (Calvin, 1996; Damasio, 1994).

In his essays documenting the experiences of those with neurological or perceptual disorders, Oliver Sacks (1995) has helped clarify this idea. In a study of Virgil, a middle-aged man who regained sight through a new surgical procedure after a lifetime of blindness, Sacks shows that one's history of learning how to see becomes integral to the organization of memory and experience. Although Virgil's surgery was successful, and he was able to physiologically "see" following the procedure, what he perceived was the visual equivalent of "noise." In order for Virgil to discern faces and objects in his visual field, he needed to learn to discard most of this visual noise. In addition, Virgil needed to re-interpret his memories, since the addition of new visual images meant a required revision of the past. This was exhausting and, in many ways debilitating. After several years, Virgil eventually became "agnosic"—psychically blind.

Interrupting familiarity is exhausting. That is why learning is

Enlarging the Space of the Possible

such hard work. This is not merely a psychological or social phenomenon—it is a biological one. Any time the brain is asked to learn something new it uses many times more physical energy than usual. Thinking requires fuel. Learning to accommodate to new understanding requires much more. This is one reason why traveling to new places creates daily exhaustion for the traveler. It is why my partner and I choose to go to the same location by the sea and rent the same cabin each year. While we want to become removed from the pressures of daily work life, we do not want to be challenged with the energy-sapping task of having to learn to negotiate a new setting.

This also helps to explain why many readers choose to read a steady stream of romance, mystery, or crime novels, and why the most popular television shows are soap operas, police or hospital dramas, or situation comedies. While the players and settings change, each of these genres is developed around specific and well-known plot structures. In order to be entertained, it seems that our perceptions must not be overly taxed or challenged. This does not mean that learning does not occur, nor does it mean that these activities should be discouraged. It does suggest, however, that an exclusive menu of such activities can create fixed boundaries for one's perceptions, reducing possibilities for the enlarging experiences that have the potential to condition the development of new insights. Involvement in formulaic experiential structures only makes small challenges to perception, while involvement in more unfamiliar structures becomes a much larger perceptual challenge.

The significant differences between small and large challenges to perception can be understood by examining the shoe activity. In thinking about this activity, it is important to note that I do not ask students to write about their own shoes. I do not do so because, in most cases, students would not be able to detach the shoe from its remembered histories and, as well, because a familiar shoe evokes nostalgia, not insight. I ask students to examine other people's *shoes*, because old shoes are intimate artifacts that reveal the trace of one human's history. In noticing the marks of wear and the dirt embedded in creases, the interpreter feels as though the intimate world of another human is being presented. At the same time, by including this artifact in the middle of one's own present life, the interpreter feels watched. This is why the collection of shoes at the Holocaust Museum in Washington D.C., piled in glass walled rooms on either side of a hallway that all visitors must pass through, is such an emotionally charged experience. Shoes collect the biological and phenomenological traces of their owners and so become intimate artifacts of history and memory. As Anne Michaels (1996) explains in *Fugitive Pieces* "It's a strange relationship that we have with objects that belonged to the dead; in the knit of atoms, their touch is left behind (p.265).

September, 2001, Edmonton, Alberta. I am revising some writing and thinking about the attack on the World Trade Center in New York City and the Pentagon in Washington, D.C. All week, I have been watching the effects of this disaster, including the rescue and recovery efforts. As nations around the world conduct rituals of mourning, I am reminded that the boundaries erected around human experiences are merely heuristic conveniences. As national anthems and songs of remembrance are sung, as prayers are recited, as eulogies are given, I am reminded of the importance of shared forms and rituals. I remember what I learned at my Catholic Retreat. I understand again why my "old shoes" activity is interesting. I am more convinced than ever of the value of shared interpretive projects, especially those that ask human beings to imagine what exists outside the familiarity of perception.

CHAPTER SEVEN

CHAPTER EIGHT

Does literature still matter? If this question asks whether most people willingly read literary texts, then it probably does not. It seems that developing one's Internet skills is considered more crucial than developing one's literary skills. And that is fine, of course. I do not intend to argue that literature will continue to matter if more people could be encouraged to read it. Instead, I would like to conclude this book by suggesting that literature matters not because *most* people read it but because *some* people read it and *some* people write it.

Whether attention is paid to readers or writers, it is true that most people believe that literature *should* matter. This belief is nurtured in school settings where literature is studied. My own critical literary education began in high schools where, like most students of my era, I was taught "close reading" practices. This meant identifying literary qualities of texts and representing their intended meanings. Studying literature meant paying attention to the details that distinguished literature from "not literature" and, at the same time, noticing the distinctions and similarities between characters and situations within a literary work, and across literary works. There was particular attention given to genre, and with the ways in which different genres evolved over historical periods.

My decision to major in English in my undergraduate liberal arts degree did not so much emerge from a love of studying literature as it did from the fact that I found the work of literary analysis easy. (I should mention, here, that finding it easy did not mean that I was considered an excellent student, merely that I could do the required work without much effort. Writing essays about Shakespeare's plays, for example, could be accomplished by following fairly simple procedures.)

Engaging in these critical close reading practices can foster a love of literature for some people, but this was not the case for me. While I was learning to conduct literary analysis, I maintained my non-academic literary engagement practices—mostly best-selling novels that were never on any of my university reading lists.

What continues to be interesting to me is that these two literary worlds seemed to remain quite distinct. I do not recall thinking that I should subject those wonderfully entertaining popular novels to any sort of close reading, nor did I think that my engagements with Shakepeare's plays should be considered anything but a school reading assignment. Literary fictions read for school purposes, then, were considered by me to be akin to reading my sociology or psychology textbook: I read in order to prepare for class seminars and to develop analyses for papers I was assigned to write.

It bears mentioning that although I did not know it then, I am now convinced that these close reading practices were useful to me. By being asked to attend to details of the text (the repeated phrases and images, the structure of sentences and paragraphs, the choice of descriptive vocabulary) I learned to attend to details outside of my engagement with text. As well, these close reading practices taught me that familiarity obscures detail. In order to notice the printed words, I needed to read passages a number of times.

In addition to learning to read slowly and to re-read, my literary education required interpretive assistance from teachers. My favorite seminars were those in which the professor spent the entire class conducting an in-depth textual analysis. From these professors I learned that a few sentences from a text, when examined closely with someone who knew how to do this work, could be like participating in what I imagined to be the experience of working in an archeological dig. If one kept looking, one would eventually find something of interest that needed interpreting. However, recognizing details and developing insight from these details are not identical experiences. While I eventually learned to craft critical essays expounding upon the qualities of literary works, I do not recall developing much personal insight from these practices.

Curiously, however, insight was generated from the attentive reading skills I learned as a drama student. For one of my studio performance classes I took the role of Sir Andrew Aguecheek in our department's production of *Twelfth Night*. While I would never have believed it possible during my study of Shakespeare's plays in English literature classes, I found that I was able to memorize large amounts of unusual dialogue without much difficulty. What interested me then was what all actors know: the ability to memorize dialogue depends upon the frequent repeating of lines within rehearsal and performance contexts. That is why it can be a disaster when one character forgets a line, since it is the memory cue for other actors. Or why it is that directors are reluctant to change a character's movements on stage once a play opens, since this can and does interrupt the structure of memory that assists with accurate line delivery.

What I found curious at the time was that one could actually memorize lines—and, it seems, effectively produce them on cue—without any sort of deep understanding of what the words meant. Even though part of the process of rehearsal included a great deal of collaborative interpretive work with the Director, there were still moments during my role as Sir Andrew Aguecheek when I was merely reciting syllables rather than engaging in some deeper meaning-making activity. I can recall, however, one night when my reciting of lines was transformed into insight. Although I can no longer remember the specific details of this event, several weeks into our run I suddenly understood what was at stake in an interaction my character was having with Sir Toby. Unfortunately, my epiphany almost immediately altered my understanding of my own character and, as I recall, created some difficulties for me (and my fellow actors) for the rest of the performance.

This is not news to anyone who has participated in repeated performances of any stage play. After all, memorizing lines written by someone else means that one, literally, is living within the structures of other people's thinking. This does not become immediately significant since it is possible to memorize a text without deeply understanding (or even really noticing) how these details might become interesting. It is only through repetitions of this structure that bridges are built between these memorized words, their relationships to other character's dialogue, and to one's remembered experiences.

As I explained in previous chapters, I have come to think of the experience of developing a deep relationship with a literary text as a focal practice—an interpretive event that occurs when one becomes committed to the making of something that provokes attention to detail, requires the development of interpretation and production skills, and sustains attention, energy and interest. As an undergraduate student, one of my focal practices was developed around the plays in which I became involved. Although I continued to study a number of literary texts and read others for non-school purposes, I would not say that these were focal practices, since I did not feel committed to them in ways that gathered my energies and interests so that insights that mattered to me could be created.

As I developed in Chapter Five, my literary encounters with Anne Michaels' (1996) novel *Fugitive Pieces* have reminded me of the importance of focal practices for people whose lives become suddenly interrupted and fragmented. Although most of us have not experienced the tragedies portrayed in this novel, like its characters we are continually challenged to interpret relationships among what we hold in memory, what we experience daily, and what we imagine as our future. In addition, we continue to interpret an understanding of our ancestors, particularly our parents or immediate childhood caregivers.

CHAPTER EIGHT

This is particularly true in a country like Canada with a history of immigration supported by what has become known as "accomodationist" cultural sensibilities. Since Confederation in 1867, Canadians have endeavored to invent what we think might be a Canadian identity while, at the same time, to remember, represent, and celebrate our collective ethnic, cultural, and linguistic differences. That our Canadian-ness might be located in our uncertainty about what this might really mean, in my view, should be considered a positive interpretive challenge. In Canada, we do not look for what might be considered the quintessential Canadian identity in grand nationalist narratives. Instead, we poke through the small details of our diverse and idiosyncratic relationships with histories, languages, and contexts in order to find our identities. This does not mean that Canadians do not have a sense of what it means to be a Canadian. What it does mean, however, is that this sense of identity continues to shift as we move across the country, across personal and local histories and experiences, and through time.

A shifting of sense of national identity is not unique to Canada and to Canadians. That people experience the relationships among ethnicity, geography, language, gender, sexuality, and nationhood differently is hardly news. This understanding of the relationships between experience and identity is also part of the narrative of what it means to be a citizen of the United States. However, the gap between the personal experiences of identity and the narratives of what it means to be American is large for many American citizens. Dominant nationalist narratives and associated images are largely organized by the imperatives to develop personal wealth, to project physical beauty and charisma, and to demonstrate an unflinching optimism about one's self and one's situation. These qualities have assisted Americans with the project of continuing to reinvent themselves. America is justifiably proud of what it has been able to create in a relatively short period of time. However, the large narratives that organize these achievements are the same ones that can create a very tiny category of possibility for many individuals, especially for those who cannot hope, through their personal efforts, to overcome their own inherited physiological traits or social circumstances.

To some degree, Canadians also experience this dissonance, particularly since they are strongly influenced by the United States. However, because the narrative of what it means to be Canadian is not so grand, the gap between ideal forms and personal experience is much smaller. It's simply easier to strive for ideal forms when those forms are ambiguously described. It is also somewhat easier when it is understood that identity is tied to land and weather. Anyone who travels across Canada knows that there is a national preoccupation with climate. My stepfather always begins telephone conversations by asking about the weather in my city and providing details about the weather in his. When I moved to Vancouver, the most common comment from my prairie friends was "but how will you be able to stand all that rain?" When I moved back to the northern prairies after several years in central Canada, my colleagues wondered, "How will you tolerate those long winters"?

In addition to the national preoccupation with weather, Canadians have always been aware of the importance of language. That Canadians continue to struggle with what it means to have two official national languages (French and English) in a country where most bilingual Canadians do not speak French and English, but English and some other language, means that the question of "what language does" is continually in the foreground. In ongoing national debates surrounding a proposed separation of the primarily French-speaking province of Quebec from the rest of the country, Canadians are asked to think about how using one language is not the same as using another. When the Québeçois insist they are a distinct society, and want constitutional guarantees that this distinctness will be acknowledged and protected in law and policy, what they are communicating is that they want their way of representing experience protected.

This has also been the case for many Canadian Aboriginal peoples who, in recent years, have worked to preserve and, in some cases, resurrect indigenous languages. An understanding of the importance of the particularity of vocabulary to represent the subtleties of personal and cultural experience is deeply woven into the Canadian cultural psyche. I would suggest that the attention to issues of language has helped Canadians to understand how important one's language is to the ongoing development of personal and cultural identities and, as well, how crucial it is to find ways to "remember" one's attachments to linguistic markers of experience.

Such attention to language may be one of the reasons that contemporary Canadian fiction tends to be interested in addressing the small but significant ways that human identities are made and changed through learned representation practices. In Ondaatje's (1992) novel *The English Patient*, readers become involved with the way four strangers learn to form a community by engaging in interpretation practices, including the reading of the English Patient's Commonplace Book. While his Commonplace Book does not reveal the identity he claimed before his involvement with the other characters, it represents the idea that knowledge cannot be finally pinned down as Truth, but can only be considered information that helps people continue to adapt to situations as they arise.

My research into literary engagement has convinced me that accomplished novelists understand the importance of attending to and representing the usually unnoticed experiences that combine to make a life. That is one reason that their novels resist being skimmed. One simply cannot appreciate the texture of *The English Patient* or *Fugitive Pieces* by racing over and through vocabulary, hunting for the overarching plot. Readers of these novels must read slowly, paying attention to the topography of the text, the texture of the interweaving plots.

Over the last century, the novel has become one vehicle for exploring the complexities and particularities of human experience. Perhaps most boldly heralded by Virginia Woolf's experiments with form, the contemporary novel has become an interpretive genre able to represent how experience is always larger than the forms used to represent it. Three prominent members of the Canadian literati—Margaret Laurence, Carol Shields, and Margaret Atwood—have each created works of literary fiction that offer insightful depictions of the way human identities are always organized by the narratives that are used to describe and explain them. In developing novels around three aging female characters [Hagar Shipley in *The Stone Angel* (Laurence, 1995[1964], Daisy Stone, *In The Stone Diaries* (Shields, 1993), and Iris Chase Griffen in *The Blind Assassin* (Atwood, 2000)], these writers provide readers with an opportunity to notice that life is not an achievement, but instead is an ongoing interpretive project. That these novels condition such insights for readers is one reason they have been so critically acclaimed. The idea that in changing one's circumstances and/or one's mind one is changing one's identity is both troubling and reassuring. In showing readers how characters work through this paradox, these writers create a literary space that is pedagogical.

It seems, then, that literary engagement can be helpful for readers. But what about writers? What prompts them to engage in the difficult work of creating literary texts? For most writers, it is not financial remuneration that propels their efforts. Very few literary writers are able to fashion a livelihood from their craft. Most writers have other jobs that pay the mortgage. My reading of the autobiographies and biographies of writers has confirmed for me that writers write because they are interested in what the practice of writing helps them to learn. While readers are usually only aware of the creative product, writers are also aware of what making the product also produces. It seems that the creation of literary characters and plots becomes a way for writers to develop new awareness of their personal situations.

My recent re-reading of James King's (1997) biography of Margaret Laurence, for example, convinced me that Laurence found writing a necessary interpretation practice. I do not mean to suggest that she always benefited positively from her writing or that she found it easy. For Laurence, the act of creating literary fiction was often excruciatingly difficult, particularly since the products of her work needed to become available for critical scrutiny. Biographers who take as their challenge the interpreting of lives through various archival and critical interpretation practices report similar experiences (DeSalvo, 1996; Grosskurth, 1999; Salvio, 1999). The dedicated and focused attention given to someone else's life can create possibilities where one's own situation is understood with greater clarity.

This is not a sensibility that is commonly understood. To some degree most of us believe that we will come to a deeper understanding of ourselves by reflecting directly on our own experience. Introspection is considered the way to personal enlightenment. However, if we consider the fact that most people are interested in hearing gossip about other people, and continue to be fascinated by other people's problems such as those that are represented on certain popular television programs, this commonsense belief becomes undermined. It seems that most people do not derive personal insight by studying themselves but, instead, do so by studying the details of other people's experience—with particular attention to how those experiences appear when used as the projection screen for their own.

This is precisely what the novelist, the poet, the playwright, the biographer, is up to when he or she creates new work. In crafting literary identities and situations, the writer needs to pay attention to the details of a world that is not of her or his own past experience or making. All writers must engage in long processes of research in order to piece together the fragments of personal and other information that eventually becomes represented as a fictional or biographical character. As Anne Michaels (1996) represents in the title of her novel, it is the writer's task to create something new from the "fugitive pieces" of personal, family, and cultural memory, and of present experiences.

In order to invent these new forms of writing, writers must find ways to interrupt the familiarity of their own experiences. However, this does not mean that writers need to sequester themselves in exotic and private locations. While some writers may in fact do this, most of the writers I know do not. Instead, they try to create conditions for creative work that largely exists in the middle of what is considered ordinary and humdrum to nonwriters. And when I say creative work, I do mean *work*. As any writer will attest, creating something from fugitive pieces means engaging in daily interpretation practices. For most writers, these include a set of routines and rituals that are designed to both interrupt the familiarity of perception and to organize insights gained from these into new forms. Alongside the techniques and skills that are necessary to good writing, these interpretation practices eventually yield products that seem inevitable yet, prior to their completion, are unpredictable. Most writers of fiction explain that they do not usually know the shape and trajectory of their work until near the end of the process.

CHAPTER EIGHT

This is why literature still matters. Literature is a product that is created by people who make it their business to interrupt the familiarity of their own perception and interpretations of the way the world "really is." In leading lives that permit literary fiction to be created, writers develop insights that are important to those who do not write.

As a former public school teacher and a working teacher educator, I am concerned that public schools are not very interested in helping young people develop the sorts of interpretation practices that I think are important. In schools, studying literature continues to mean reading a lot of it rather quickly and being able to identify literary devices and write critical essays. While in recent years there has been increased attention to the teaching of writing, in many cases writing is not being taught by writers. This is one reason that, if asked, most young people would say that neither reading nor writing literature matters. In order for literature to matter, it needs to be considered an integral feature of human experience. In addition to creating funding for persons to develop their interests in literary work, we need to reconsider what it means to include this work in schools.

Of course, there are also problems with how literature is read outside of school contexts. Too often, literary engagement is considered some sort of pleasurable activity that requires nothing other than a willingness to let oneself be absorbed by an aesthetic experience. This is why so many readers abandon great novels such as Ondaatje's (1992) *The English Patient*, or Urquhart's (1997) *The Underpainter.* Novels such as these are written in forms that exist slightly outside the boundaries of how most readers think that novels should be written. And, because most of what counts as reading is a projection of what the reader thinks the text should say, it is not surprising that many readers become impatient with one that asks them, first, to try to notice the topography of the text before drawing conclusions about how they must engage with it. Because most readers do not consider reading literature an interpretation practice, it is simply inconceivable to many that they should have to learn how to have a relationship with a text.

As I explained earlier, one does not need to be a reader or a writer of literature to gain insights. However, one does need some sort of interpretation practice that takes one outside the boundaries of what is considered commonsense understanding. For example, from my own limited experience in the theatre, and from what I have heard and read of experienced actors and directors, the insights gained from becoming immersed, over an extended period of time, in other peoples' thinking and circumstances, can be profound. Memorizing lines that someone else has written, becoming immersed in the situation of a character, over time, can help one to escape one's own familiar perceptions, and enter into a critical engagement with the circumstances of one's personal and cultural biographies.

As a teacher and teacher educator, I understand that most of my students will not become professional writers of fiction or biography. Most of them will not develop insights about their own lives through deep engagements with literary fictions after they leave my classroom. They will not be able to escape what is considered commonsense understanding through sustained practices of writing. Some of my students publicly announce (without any embarrassment) that they don't read fiction all and are only doing it in my class because it is a "requirement." I am not bothered by these confessions, since I understand that my job as a teacher is not to try to control what my students do outside the boundaries of pedagogies I offer but, instead, to offer interesting experiences within those boundaries that might have a lingering effect. As is evident from what I have written in previous chapters, I have some practices that have become favourites.

CHAPTER EIGHT

In all the courses I teach, I ask students to pay attention to the representational forms we are studying. I do this in very traditional ways by asking them for close readings of texts we read (both literary fiction and other texts). I also ask them to become involved with the forms we are reading by copying out passages verbatim several times. In so doing I am hoping that they might be able to get inside the mind of the author who has created this form, in much the same way that I felt I was able to get inside my character Andrew Aguecheek by repeating memorized lines over and over. I also ask my students to represent their own experiences by copying the syntax of favorite prose and fiction passages. In trying to represent personal experience with someone else's writing structures, students gain new insight.

These are all reading and writing practices I consider to be variations of literary practices that I know many writers of fiction use. I do not ask my students to engage in them because I think this will help them to become novelists or poets (although it might, and that would be nice). I do so because I think it helps them to experience what is necessary to reconsider what they think to be true about their personal worlds of experience. One does not learn, deeply, about one's own experience by studying that experience directly, but rather, one learns about personal experience by studying it in the ways I have suggested—obliquely.

The practices I use are ones that create conditions for the development of deep insight. I use the structures that I do because they are the ones that I like, and have learned to use with some degree of skill. I know, however, that there are many ways to condition this sort of critical imagination. I do not believe that everyone should be interested in using literary engagement as an interpretation practice. However, I do believe that everyone should have some focal practice that helps her or him make sense of experience. Some people write novels. Other people paint pictures. Other people are expert gardeners. No matter what the practices, involvement in them asks participants to pay attention to certain details (and not others), and this contributes strongly to how they understand themselves, their relations with others, and their contexts. Most of these practices will not be taught in public schools (at least not as part of the official curriculum). They will not be taught because schools ask that students learn to represent and reproduce commonsense. And there is more commonsense than ever to be learned, it seems. The time and energy of public education is largely devoted to having students project what is already known, not to invent new ways of knowing.

This is why literature does not matter much to those who associate literature with what happens in schools. In order for literature to matter in school, one must abandon theories of learning that insist on excavating Truth, or representing commonsense. This means creating conditions for people to learn to be surprised by what might happen if they dedicated themselves to literary practices that require a sustained engagement with someone else's structure of thinking. As I have argued throughout this book, literary engagement ought to be considered an interesting way for people to develop insight that matters to themselves, and that might also matter to other people. Some people will create these insights by writing literature. Others will create insights through interpretive reading practices. The rest will benefit because this work has been done.

CHAPTER EIGHT

References

161

Abram, D. (1996). *The spell of the sensuous: Perception and language in a more than human world.* New York: Pantheon Books.

Als, H. (1997). *The women.* New York: Farrar, Straus, Giroux.

Alvermann, D., & Hruby, G. (2000). Mentoring and reporting research: A concern for aesthetics. *Reading Research Quarterly, 35,* 46–63.

Appleyard, J.A. (1990). *Becoming a reader: The experience of fiction from childhood to adulthood.* New York: Cambridge University Press.

Atwood, M. (2000). *The blind assassin.* Toronto: McClelland & Stewart.

Bateson, M-C. (1994). *Peripheral visions: Learning along the way.* New York: HarperCollins.

Beach, R. (1993). *A teacher's introduction to reader-response theories.* Urbana, IL: National Council of Teachers of English.

Beach, R. (2000). Reading and responding to literature at the level of activity. *Journal of Literacy Research, 32,* 237–252.

Beach, R., & Myers, J. (2001). *Inquiry-Based English instruction: Engaging students in life and literature.* New York: Teachers College Press.

Behar, R. (1996). *The vulnerable observer: Anthropology that breaks your heart.* Boston: Beacon Press.

Bhaba, H. (1990). *Nation and narrative.* London: Routledge.

Bleich, D. (1978). *Subjective criticism.* Baltimore: The Johns Hopkins University Press.

Borgmann, A. (1992). *Crossing the postmodern divide.* Chicago: The University of Chicago Press.

Britzman, D. (1998). *Lost subjects, contested objects: Toward a psychoanalytic inquiry of learning.* Albany, NY: State University of New York Press.

Brockman, J. (Ed.). (1995). *The third culture: Beyond the scientific revolution.* New York: Simon & Schuster.

Brooks, M. (1997). *Bone dance.* Toronto: Groundwood Books.

Bruner, J. (1986). *Actual minds, possible worlds.* Cambridge, MA: Harvard University Press.

Bruner, J. (1990). *Acts of meaning.* Cambridge, MA: Harvard University Press.

Butala, S. (1994). *The perfection of the morning: An apprenticeship in nature.* Toronto: HarperCollins.

Calvin, W. (1996). *How brains think: Evolving intelligence, then and now.* New York: Basic Books.

Capra, F. (1996). *The web of life: A new scientific understanding of living systems.* New York: Penguin Books.

Clark, A. (1996). *Being there: Putting brain, body, and world together again.* Cambridge, MA: The MIT Press.

Clifford, J., & Marcus, G. (Eds.). (1986). *Writing culture: The poetics and politics of ethnography*. Los Angeles: University of California Press.

Cohen, J., & Stewart, I. (1994). *The collapse of chaos: Discovering simplicity in a complex world*. New York: Penguin Books.

Culler, J. (1997). *Literary theory*. Oxford: Oxford University Press.

Damasio, A. (1994). *Descartes' error: Emotion, reason, and the human brain*. New York: G.P. Putnam Sons.

Davis, B., Sumara, D., & Luce-Kapler, L. (2000). *Engaging minds: Learning and teaching in a complex world*. Mahwah, NJ: Lawrence Erlbaum Associates.

Deacon, T. (1997). *The symbolic species: The co-evolution of language and the brain*. New York: W.W. Norton & Company.

Denzin, N., & Lincoln, Y. (Eds.). (1994). *Handbook of qualitative research*. Thousand Oaks, CA: Sage Publications.

Derrida, J. (1976). *Of grammatology*. Baltimore: The Johns Hopkins University Press.

Derrida, J. (1978). *Writing and différance*. London: Routledge.

Derrida, J. (1992). *Acts of literature*. New York: Routledge.

DeSalvo, L. (1996). *Vertigo*. New York: Dutton.

DeSalvo, L. (1997). *Breathless: An asthma journal*. Boston: Beacon Press.

Dewey, J. (1996). *Democracy and education*. New York: The Free Press. (Original work published 1916.)

Doll. M.A. (2000). *Like letters in running water: A mythopoetics of curriculum*. Mahwah, NJ: Lawrence Erlbaum Associates.

Dowling, J. (1998). *Creating mind: How the brain works*. New York: W.W. Norton.

Eco, U. (1994). *Six walks in the fictional woods*. Cambridge: Harvard University Press.

Egan, K. (1997). *The educated mind: How cognitive tools shape our understanding*. Chicago: University of Chicago Press.

Ellsworth, E. (1997). *Teaching positions: Difference, pedagogy, and the power of address*. New York: Teachers College Press.

Fish, S. (1980). *Is there a text in this class?* Cambridge, MA: Harvard University Press.

Flax, J. (1990). *Thinking fragments: Psychoanalysis, feminism and postmodernism in the contemporary west*. Berkeley: University of California Press.

Fox, M. (1985). *Wilfrid Gordon McDonald Partridge*. Brooklyn: Kane/Miller.

Foucault, M. (1972). *The archeology of knowledge*. New York: Pantheon Books.

Foucault, M. (1988). Technologies of the self. In M. Luther, H. Gutman, &

P. Hutton (Eds.), *Technologies of the self: A seminar with Michel Foucault* (pp. 16–49). Amherst, MA: University of Massachusetts Press.

Fulford, R. (1999). *The triumph of narrative: Storytelling in the age of mass culture.* Toronto: Anansi.

Gadamer, H-G. (1976). *Philosophical hermeneutics.* Los Angeles: University of California Press.

Gadamer, H-G. (1990). *Truth and method.* New York: Crossroad.

Gallop, J. (2000). The ethics of close reading: Close encounters. *Journal of Curriculum Theorizing, 17*(3), 7–17.

Gay, P. (1998). *My German question: Growing up in Nazi Berlin.* New Haven, CT: Yale University Press.

Geertz, C. (1988). *Works and lives: Anthropologist as author.* Stanford, CA: Stanford University Press.

Greene, M. (1995). *Releasing the imagination: Essays on education, the arts, and social change.* San Francisco: Jossey-Bass.

Griffin, S. (1992). *A chorus of stones: The private life of war.* New York: Doubleday.

Grossberg, L., Nelson, C., & Treichler, P. (1992). *Cultural studies.* New York: Routledge.

Grosskurth, P. (1999). *Elusive subject: A biographer's life.* Toronto: MacFarlane Walter & Ross.

Grumet, M. (1988). *Bitter milk: Women and teaching.* Amherst: University of Massachusetts Press.

Grumet, M. (1991a). Curriculum and the art of daily life. In Willis, G. & Schubert, W. (Eds), *Reflections from the heart of educational inquiry: Understanding curriculum and teaching through the arts* (pp. 74–89). Albany, NY: SUNY Press

Grumet, M. (1991b). Lost places, potential spaces and possible worlds: Why we read books with other people. *Margins, 1*(1), 35–53.

Harris, J.R. (1998). *The nurture assumption: Why children turn out the way they do.* New York: Touchstone.

Harste, J.C., Woodward, V.A., & Burke, C.L. (1984). *Language stories and literacy lessons.* Portsmouth, NH: Heinemann.

Hay, E. (2000). *A student of weather.* Toronto: McClelland & Stewart.

Heidegger, M. (1966). *Being and time.* New York: Harper and Row.

Heidegger, M. (1977). *Basic writings.* San Francisco: HarperCollins.

Herodotus. (1954). *Histories.* Middlesex, UK: Penguin Books.

Hirsch, E. (1976). *The aims of interpretation.* Chicago: The University of

Chicago Press.

Hoffman, E. (1989). *Lost in translation*. New York: Penguin Books.

Iser, W. (1975). *The implied reader*. Baltimore: The Johns Hopkins University Press.

Iser, W. (1978). *The act of reading*. Baltimore: The Johns Hopkins University Press.

Iser, W. (1989). *Prospecting: From reader response to literary anthropology*. Baltimore: The Johns Hopkins University Press.

Iser, W. (1993). *The fictive and the imaginary: Charting literary anthropology*. Baltimore: The Johns Hopkins University Press.

Iser, W. (2000). *The range of interpretation*. New York: Columbia University Press.

Johnson, M. (1997). *Developmental cognitive neuroscience: An introduction*. Cambridge, MA: Blackwell Publishers.

Kerby, A. (1991). *Narrative and the self*. Bloomington, IN: Indiana University Press.

King, J. (1997). *The life of Margaret Laurence*. Toronto: Alfred A. Knopf.

Kotulak, R. (1996). *Inside the brain: Revolutionary discoveries of how the mind works*. New York: Andrews and McMeel.

Kristeva, J. (1984). *Revolution in poetic language*. New York: Columbia University Press.

Laidlaw, L. (2001). *Travelling by text: An inquiry into writing, learning and human experience*. Unpublished Doctoral Dissertation. Toronto: York University.

Lakoff, G., & Johnson, M. (1999). *Philosophy in the flesh: The embodied mind and its challenge to western thought*. New York: Basic Books.

Langer, S. (1957). *Problems of art*. New York: Charles Scribner's Sons.

Lather, P. (1991). *Getting smart: Feminist research and pedagogy with/in the postmodern*. New York: Routledge.

Laurence, M. (1995). *The stone angel*. Toronto: McClelland & Stewart. (Original work published 1964)

Leavis, F. (1950). *New bearings in English Poetry*. London: Chatto and Windus. (Original work published 1932)

Lerner, G. (1997). *Why history matters*. New York: Oxford University Press.

Lewin, R. (1993). *The origin of modern humans*. New York: Scientific American Library.

Lewis, C. (2000). Limits of identificaiton: The personal, pleasurable, and critical in reader response. *Journal of Literacy Research. 32*, 253–266.

Lewontin, R. (2000). *It ain't necessarily so: The dream of the human genome and other illusions.* New York: New York Review Books.

Lowry, L. (1993). *The giver.* New York: Bantam Doubleday.

Luce-Kapler, R. (2000). As if women writing. *Journal of Literacy Research, 32,* 267–291.

Lyotard, J-F. (1984). *The postmodern condition: A report on knowledge.* Minneapolis: Minnesota Press.

Mackey, M. (1998). *The case of Peter Rabbit: Changing conditions of literature for children.* New York: Garland Publishing.

Maturana, H., & Varela, F. (1987). *The tree of knowledge: The biological roots of human understanding.* Boston: Shambhala.

Meek, M. (1991). *On being literate.* London: The Bodley Head.

Merleau-Ponty, M. (1962). *Phenomenology of perception.* London: Routledge & Kegan Paul.

Michaels, A. (1996). *Fugitive pieces.* Toronto: McClelland & Stewart.

Miller, J. (1990). *Creating spaces and finding voices: Teachers collaborating for empowerment.* New York: State University of New York Press.

Morris, M. (2001). *Curriculum and the Holocaust: Competing sites of memory and representation.* Mahwah, NJ: Lawrence Erlbaum Associates.

Morrison, T. (1996). *The dancing mind.* New York: Alfred A. Knopf.

Nell, V. (1988). *Lost in a book: The psychology of reading for pleasure.* New Haven, CT: Yale University Press.

Norretranders, T. (1998). *The user illusion: Cutting consciousness down to size.* Trans. J. Sydenham. New York: Viking.

Norris, K. (1993). *Dakota: A spiritual geography.* Boston: Houghton Mifflin.

Ondaatje, M. (1992). *The English patient.* Toronto: McClelland & Stewart.

Pinar, W., Reynolds, W., Slattery, P., & Taubman, P. (1995). *Understanding curriculum.* New York: Peter Lang.

Pinker, S. (1997). *How the mind works.* New York: W.W. Norton.

Rorty, R. (1989). *Contingency, irony, solidarity.* Cambridge, UK: Cambridge University Press.

Rorty, R. (1999). *Philosophy and social hope.* Toronto: Penguin Books.

Richardson, L. (1997). *Fields of play: Constructing an academic life.* New Brunswick, NJ: Rutgers University Press.

Rosenblatt, L. (1938). *Literature as exploration.* New York: Appleton Century.

Rosenblatt, L. (1978). *The reader, the text, the poem.* Carbondale, IL: Southern Illinois University Press.

Sacks, O. (1995). *An anthropologist on Mars: Seven paradoxical tales.* New York:

167

Alfred A. Knopf.

Said, E. (1993). *Culture and imperialism.* New York: Alfred A. Knopf.

Salvio, P. (1995). On the forbidden pleasures and hidden dangers of covert reading. *English Quarterly, 27*(3), 8–15.

Salvio, P. (1999). Teacher of 'weird abundance': Portraits of the pedagogical tactics of Anne Sexton. *Cultural Studies, 13*, 639–660.

Salzman, M. (2000). *Lying awake.* New York: Alfred A. Knopf.

Shields, C. (1993). *The Stone diaries.* Toronto: Random House.

Smith, D.G. (1991). Hermeneutic inquiry: The hermeneutic imagination and the pedagogic text. In E. Short (Ed.), *Forms of Curriculum Inquiry.* New York: SUNY Press.

Spivey, N. (1997). *The constructivist metaphor: Reading, writing, and the making of meaning.* San Diego: Academic Press.

Sumara, D. (1996). *Private readings in public: Schooling the literary imagination.* New York: Peter Lang.

Sumara, D., Davis, B., & van der Wey, D. (1998). The pleasure of thinking. *Language Arts, 76*(2), 135–143.

Taylor, C. (1989). *Sources of the self: The making of modern identity.* Cambridge, MA: Harvard University Press.

Thich Nhat Hahn (1991). *Peace is every step: The path of mindfulness in everyday life.* New York: Bantam Books.

Thompson, R.F. (1996). *The brain: A neuroscience primer.* New York: W.H. Freeman.

Todorov, T. (1977). *The poetics of prose.* Ithaca: Cornell University Press.

Urquhart, J. (1997). *The underpainter.* Toronto: McClelland & Stewart.

Urquhart, J. (2001). *The stone carvers.* Toronto: McClelland & Stewart.

Van Maanen, J. (1988). *Tales of the field: On writing ethnography.* Chicago: University of Chicago Press.

Varela, F., Thompson, E. & Rosch, E. (1991). *The embodied mind: Cognitive science and human experience.* Cambridge, MA: The MIT Press.

von Glasersfeld, E. (1995). *Radical constructivism: A way of knowing and learning.* London: The Falmer Press.

Willinsky, J. (1998). *Learning to divide the world: Education and the empire's end.* Minneapolis, MN: University of Minnesota Press.

Winterson, J. (1995). *Art objects: Essays on ecstasy and effrontery.* Toronto: Alfred A. Knopf.

Acknowledgments

This book represents a multi-generational project that began in Germany in the 1930s when Frances Meier Oberberger decided that her eldest daughter, Cecelia, should receive the best education possible. Through her tenacity and charisma, she organized my mother's early education at a private convent school. World War II interrupted my grandmother's plans, and led to the unexpected emigration of my mother to Canada. Although the project did not continue in ways either my grandmother or mother expected, it did continue. In large measure, this book emerges from the labor and ingenuity of these two women. Although they were not writers, they loved to read, and they knew the value of focal practices. I have appreciated and benefited from their insights.

As I argue throughout this book, ideas emerge from complex relations. The ideas I explore here are no exception. They have been created from my associations with books, with authors of books, with friends and colleagues, and with students. Although some of these influences are noted in the citations given, the depth of involvement cannot be communicated in this way. I am indebted to many people who, over the last decade, have helped me explore some of my ideas, and who have challenged me to improve my arguments.

The "JCT Conference on Curriculum Theory and Classroom Practice" and its associated *JCT: Journal of Curriculum Theorizing* created an important interpretive site for my thinking. I am grateful to Janet Miller and William Pinar, whose dedication to both the conference and the journal created necessary conditions for me and for other scholars interested in creating new forms of curriculum scholarship.

Another very influential conference has been the "National Reading Conference" and its associated *Journal of Literacy Research*. This conference and journal have provided me with a generous location to publicly present some of my ideas about literary engagement. Although many persons associated with NRC have contributed to my thinking, I would particularly like to extend my appreciation to Donna Alvermann, Jerome Harste and Richard Beach. They have not only provided intellectual assistance, but also have helped create conditions for me to improve the quality of my work.

I would not have been able to invent the ideas presented in this book without frequent and helpful exchanges with Rebecca Luce-Kapler and Brent Davis. Through work we shared on another writing project, I came to appreciate the depth of their knowledge, and I came to more clearly understand the importance of interpretation practices.

Anyone who has read the work of Madeleine Grumet and Louise DeSalvo will recognize how at times I have copied their writing styles. At first, I did not know I was doing this. However, as I re-read some of their work during the year I worked on this book, I realized that I had found my way into their thinking by learning how to live inside their sentences. I have appreciated this collaboration, even though my collaborators have been largely unaware of their participation.

At some point in the writing process, every author needs some critical friends. Linda Laidlaw and Anne Meier have been two important resources. Linda's meticulous editing and gentle (yet persistent) questioning of an early draft of this book helped me to significantly improve the quality of my thinking and writing. Anne's expert proofreading and advice smoothed many rough edges.

My colleagues told me that Naomi Silverman was one of the best editors in the business. My experience working with her through two books has confirmed this for me. In addition to smoothing the many bumps in the road to producing and publishing this manuscript, she saved me from the dreadful book titles I invented earlier in the process.

Earlier versions of some of the chapters in this book have been published elsewhere and appear with the permission of the publishers. An earlier version of Chapter Two was published in *Changing English: Studies in Reading and Culture* (volume 8, number 2). A version of Chapter Four appears in *JCT: Journal of Curriculum Theorizing* (volume 14, number 4). A version of Chapter Five appears in *Journal of Literacy Research* (volume 34, number 2). An earlier version of Chapter Seven can be found in *Educational Insights* (volume 7, number 1).

Finally, I am grateful to the Social Sciences and Humanities Research Council of Canada for generous funding that has allowed me to pursue my ideas.

Index

hermeneutics, 29–31, 89; dialectial, 30, 35
Herodotus, 19, 33
high school: experiences of, 134
Hirsch, Eric Donald, 92
history: geography and, 75, 102; identity and, 78, 89; influence of, *xiv*; memory and, 4, 26, 74, 76
Hoffman, Eva, 86
Holocaust, 74
Holocaust Museum, 143
Hruby, George, 73
human science research, 82

identification: identity and, 10, 13, 54; insight and, 33; intelligence and, 26; interpretation and, 14; literacy and, 30, 76; textual, *xiv*, 11
identity: American, 151–152; art and, 9; Canadian, 151–152; coherence and, 13, 59; commonsense and, *xvi*; creating, 9–10, 25; cultural artifacts and, 112; experiences of, 12; fixed, 58; geography and, 74, 121, 152; historical views of, 51; identification and, 10, 13, 54; imagination and, 74, 77; interpretation and, 8; knowledge and, 4; language and, *xv*, 15, 24, 140; narrative and, 115, 154; pedagogy and, 56; post-structuralism and, 89; reading and, 30, 85; representing, 63, 153; ritual and, 25–26; secrets and, 83; technology and, 26; theories of, 59
illness: creativity and, 129; experiences of, 108; writing and, 41
imagination, 5, 12, 24, 86, 135, 159; identity and, 74, 77; literary experience and, 10, 11
immigration, 90
indeterminacy: reading and, 34, 97
information: interpretation and, 36;

learning and, 111
insight, 4, 114; creating, *xiii*, 7, 19, 67, 92, 100, 102, 130, 137, 159; conditions for, 5; deep, *xiv*; interpretation and, 33; writing and, 155, 157
intelligence: identification and, 26
Internet, *xiv*, 10, 62, 124
interpretation: critical, 27; cultural, 78; historical, 78; identification and, 15; information and, 36; intergenerational, 158; intimacy and, 116; Judaism and, 32–33, 78; language and, 86; memory and, 88; practices of, *xiii*, *xiv*, 139–143; problems of, 11; trauma and, 75
interpretive community, 95
intertext, 34
intimacy: interpretation and, 116
Iser, Wolfgang, 11, 29, 32, 33, 34, 58, 94, 96–97

Johnson, Mark, 61, 65
jouissance, 133
justice: questions of, 90

Kerby, Anthony, 53
King, James, 6, 8, 155
knowledge: difficulty and, 27, 144; identity and, 4; personal, 40; reading and, 93
Kotuluk, Ronald, 66
Kristeva, Julia, 28

Laidlaw, Linda, 69
Lakoff, George, 61
landscape, 119; experience and, 79; perception and, 138; textual, 121
Langer, Suzanne, 46
language, 15, 102; consciousness and, 85; creating, 64; creativity and, 16; experience and, 87–88; geography and, 4, 79–92; identity

and, 83, 152; interpretation and, 86; memory and, 84, 86; post-structuralism and, 95, 96–97; subjunctive forms, 5; as technology, 8, 61; truth and, 8; written, 65

language arts, 21

Lather, Patti, 94

Laurence, Margaret, 3, 6, 7, 8, 154, 155

learning: beliefs about, 46, 111; biography and, 68; discernment and, 122; perception and, 138

Leavis, Frank, 92

Lerner, Gerda, 84

Lewin, Roger, 65

Lewis, Cynthia, 93

Lewontin, Richard, 66

Lincoln, Yvonna, 86

literacy, 62

literary analysis, 147–148

literary anthropology, 29, 94, 102; methods, 99–100; reader response and, 98

literary engagement, *xiv*, 9, 11–12, 28, 78, 98; definition, 98–99; identity and, 67; mindfulness and, 122; as research, 19, 58, 154; in schools, 157

literary identification: problems, 77

literary imagination, 10–11

literary interpretation, 5, 15, 44, 64

literary theory, 86, 92

literature: as art, 123; Canadian, 5; as commonplace, 97; conditions for creating, 6; as cultural artifact, 30; cultural purposes, 77, 147–160; university teaching and, 147

love: experiences of, *xvii*, 107–108, 115; happiness and, 109; hate and, 117; infatuation vs., 116; learning about, 109; popular narratives of, 107, 112; romantic, 108; of teachers 118;

Lowry, Lois, *xvi*, 20, 97

Luce-Kapler, Rebecca, 14, 69, 73, 93, 97, 136, 140

Lyotard, Jean-François, 4

Mackey, Margaret, 58

Marcus, George, 94

mathematics, 67

Maturana, Humberto, 65, 135, 137

Meek, Margaret, 24

memoir, 3

memorizing, 149; importance of, 158

memory, 3, 80, 102; aging and, 51; artifacts and, 55; coherence and, 63; cultural, 27; experience and, 141; history and, 4, 26, 74, 76, 89; interpretation and, 88, 140–141; narrative and, 52; topography and, 55

Merleau-Ponty, Maurice, 42, 82, 141

Michaels, Anne, *xiv*, *xvii*, 3, 73–76, 78–83, 85, 87–90, 102, 119, 156

Midrash: Judaic practices of, 32

Miller, Janet, 4

mind: embodied, 137

mindfulness, *xvii*, 98, 122; and discernment, 124

modernism, 110–111

Morris, Marla, 73

Morrison, Toni, 44

narrative: autobiographical, 83; experience and, 61; gossip and, 60; historical, 27; interpretation and, 87; memory and, 53, 59; nationalism and, 151; self and, 115, 152, 154; teacher education and, 117

narrative tableaux, 69

nature-nurture: debates, 65

Nazism, 75, 81, 88–89

Nell, Victor, 13

Nelson, Cary, 86
neuroscience, 65; identity and, 82
Norretranders, Tor, 66, 138
Norris, Kathleen, 124, 138
nuns: experiences with, 133–134

Ondaatje, Michael, *xvi*, 19, 76, 97, 153, 157

pedagogy, *xiii*, 28, 103, 118–119, 154; adolescence and, 56; identity and, 56; memory and, 68; practices, 138
peer group: identity formation and, 57
perception, 40, 127; changing, 112; interrupting, *xvi*, 9, 143; learning and, 138; neurological research and, 141; problems with, 141–142; understanding and, 3
phenomenology: biology and, 129
philosophy: Continental, 86; Eastern, 137; pragmatist, 28–29, 86, 92
Pinar, William, 86
Pinker, Steven, 138
place: sense of, 6, 79
poetry: reading, 40
Poland, 74–75
post-structuralism, 28, 89; language and, 94, 96–97
pragmatism: philosophical, 28–29, 86, 92
psychoanalysis, 86

Québec, 153

reader-response, xiv, 14–15, 24, 33; literary anthropology and, 98; practices, 22, 29; research and, 13; theory, 92–93
reading: adults' experiences, 97; aesthetic, 93; archive and, 23; children's experiences, 97; close, *xiv*, 120–122, 124, 148, 154, 159;

context and, 11, 24; efferent, 93; embodied, *xvii*; experiences of, 5, 158; familiarity and, 142; identification and, 91; identity and, 30, 54, 85; indeterminacy and, 94, 97; interpretation and, 31, 91; oral, 58; physical effects of, 43; popular, 142; in schools, 33; shared, 58
Reason, 110
relationship: literary, 95; pedagogical, 118–119
representation: art and, 9; experience and, 7
re-reading, 39, 76, 101–102, 148; effects of, 6; practices of, 19, 22; purposes for, 80; in schools, 150; significance of, 122–123
research: fictionalizing and, 94; human science, *xvii*; teacher, 36
Reynolds, William, 86
Richardson, Laurel, 67, 76, 94
ritual: Catholic, *xviii*, 127–128; effects of, 25–26; grieving and, 13; identity and, 131; literary practices and, 136; writing and, 156
Rorty, Richard, 4, 15, 16, 28, 77, 78, 90, 96, 102
Rosch, Eleanor, 93, 137
Rosenblatt, Louise, 11, 24, 33, 34, 92–93

Sacks, Oliver, 138, 141
Said, Edward, 26
Salvio, Paula, 60, 76, 155
Salzman, Mark, *xviii*, 127, 129
schooling, *xiii*, 33, 56
secrets: effects of, 113–115; identity and, 83
sex, 107
sexuality, 116
Shakespeare, William, 148–149
Shields, Carol, 154
Slattery, Patrick, 86

175

INDEX